# Back to Bizkaia

THE BASQUE SERIES

# Back to Bizkaia

## A BASQUE-AMERICAN MEMOIR

## Vince J. Juaristi

University of Nevada Press

RENO AND LAS VEGAS

THE BASQUE SERIES

University of Nevada Press, Reno, Nevada 89557 USA
Copyright © 2011 by Vince J. Juaristi
All rights reserved
Manufactured in the United States of America
Design by Kathleen Szawiola

*Library of Congress Cataloging-in-Publication Data*

Juaristi, Vince J., 1969–
Back to Bizkaia : a Basque-American memoir / Vince J. Juaristi.
p.   cm. — (The Basque series)
ISBN 978-0-87417-859-3 (pbk. : alk. paper)
1. Juaristi, Joe, 1930–   2. Juaristi, Joe, 1930–   —Travel—Spain—País Vasco.
3. Juaristi, Vince J., 1969–   Travel—Spain—País Vasco. 4. País Vasco (Spain)—
Travel and description.  5. Fathers and sons—United States—Biography.
6. Basque Americans—Biography. I. Title.
E184.B15J83 2011
946'.6—dc22              2011012652

The paper used in this book is a recycled stock made from 30 percent
post-consumer waste materials, certified by FSC, and meets
the requirements of American National Standard for Information
Sciences—Permanence of Paper for Printed Library Materials,
ANSI/NISO Z39.48-1992 (R2002).
Binding materials were selected for strength and durability.

FIRST PRINTING
20   19   18   17   16   15   14   13   12   11
5   4   3   2   1

————✺————

*To Dad and Mom*
*who made a fine home*
*for us kids in America*

# Preface

I needed to tell a story, and the story turned into a book. This book is about a surprise trip that I made with my seventy-eight-year-old father to his native Basque Country in 2008. Dad had first left Spain in 1948 to escape Francisco Franco's repressive government, but now a timely return was important—his twin sister was in a nursing home, sinking into the dark depths of Alzheimer's disease, and other siblings and friends, aging and fragile, had far fewer days ahead of them than behind.

As I wrote about this journey, I realized that I needed to tell two other stories. One was about Dad's life after he left Spain and arrived in Elko, Nevada, to make his new home. Here the poor boy from Gizaburuaga, Spain, became a successful businessman and sheepherder, established a family, and became part of Elko's large Basque community. The second story was my own—that of a second-generation Basque American who grew up struggling with his roots and longing to explore the larger world beyond Elko's comfortable streets. Our trip to Euskadi brought Dad and me together in ways we had never experienced before, and it gave me a far deeper understanding of my Old Country connection.

In some ways, this is the story of a single immigrant's return to his Basque origins. On another level, it is every immigrant's story—the return to a homeland that has changed over the years and to family and friends who have changed as well. It is also the story of every immigrant's American-born child, seeing the land of his ancestors through his own eyes and those of the returning parent. It is a Basque story—and a uniquely American story.

The telling of the story did not come without challenges. The spice of any manuscript derives from subtlety—the use of one word over another, the twist of phrase, the memorable nature of a story. In a book that cobbles together bits and pieces from three languages an expression of subtlety becomes a daunting challenge. For me, it created three problems, which I endeavored to mitigate in nearly every sentence.

The first challenge came in the use of Spanish and Basque names. In Euskadi, for example, each town or city, landmark or church, has a Spanish name and a Basque name. Initially, I applied a single rule—to use only Basque names—but ended up sacrificing the general familiarity that many people have gained over the years of various locations and landmarks in the Basque Country. I decided, therefore, to use only Spanish names, but then I feared I might offend the Basques themselves who speak of their beloved towns and churches and landmarks mostly in their native tongue and grow weary of others who resort so quickly to Spanish. In the end, I applied no rule, but remained conscientious about when and where I used Basque or Spanish names throughout the manuscript. In some instances, I included both. If anyone gets confused or becomes offended, please forgive me, and know that I tried my best to avoid both circumstances.

The second challenge came from translations. I represented all dialogues between me and Dad verbatim. Not many can understand Dad, but I can. I've often joked that I'm his English-to-English translator, able to boil down complex material to bare-bone simplicity, both for his comprehension and for the comprehension of others. For all other dialogues, I relied on my own understanding of the languages, or on on-the-spot translations from Dad or a cousin or a friend in the room. In all of these cases, I sought immediate feedback to preserve the moment, the joy, the anger, the exact phrase where possible. No doubt a sentiment was skewed along the way, subtlety got lost, and spice grew bland, but the overall meaning remained true to the best of my ability.

The last challenge came from the fragility of memory. The book offers recollections both from me as a boy and from Dad as a younger man. Time chips away at memory, burns it, changes it. Events seem bigger or smaller, the fish grows in length, the poignant emotion fades. In each telling of a story, Dad offers variations of color and texture, dialogue and detail, and characters gain or lose a trait, but in all cases the core of the stories—the lesson or the significant point—stays true. To reconcile these variations, I sifted through the multiple versions and settled on one.

Finally, no one has truly researched or conducted an interview until one tries to decipher and understand the starts and stops and occasional ramblings of an old Basque sheepherder. But if one listens closely, one finds joy in the experience. Where clarity falls short, wisdom rises up.

# Back to Bizkaia

# 1

I deceived everyone.

Sister Mary Kathleen's ghost towered over me, looking sternly German, to declare my deception an outright lie. Her spiritual counterpart, Sister Dennis, a soft, chubby redheaded Irish nun with rosy cheeks, agreed and then warmly hugged me. Early in life, these two had lined my moral high road with psychic barbed wire so that any straying caused prickly pain and eventually confession. They saw only black and white, good and bad. The devil played in the gray.

Despite risk to my immortal soul, I worked to conceal my deception. I practiced in front of a mirror so the words came out smoothly without a hint of subterfuge or nerves. Whenever anyone asked a question, I used muffled tones, spoke with a lazy tongue as if I had had a stroke, or walked outside with the deception trailing behind me as the door slammed shut. Professional prevaricators no doubt found my tactics amateurish, but I did the best I could under the weight of a nagging and defiant conscience, a permanent gift from those lovely nuns of St. Joseph's Catholic Church in Elko, Nevada.

Family and friends didn't recognize the signs. No one had reason to suspect me. My reputation shined with unvarnished truth. They knew that about me and relied on it like Gibraltar's rock, as guide and landmark through stormy weather. My deception bordered therefore on betrayal, not of family and friends but of my trademark of speaking honestly and simply with others, of being that permanent fixture on whom others leaned for strength and reassurance.

I'm sure this admission makes me sound like a bad guy. Some might condemn me to burn in eternal fire. I hope not. My deception served a greater purpose. The good sisters had said that deception in any form for any reason must not be tolerated. But I knew the heart to be self-policing, that God had allowed deception, told us to be gentle as doves and wise as serpents. I took this as license to deceive only rarely, and then only for a greater purpose.

Such reasoning I knew echoed in history. Nefarious characters had justified their evil ways by pointing to benevolent ends. Historians with centuries of hindsight had later concluded smugly that ends do not justify means. True—in most cases.

But my case was different. No one died, no one got hurt, no one lost money. No one became the wiser until after the event passed.

My deception to Mom and sisters, aunts, uncles, and cousins benefited one person—Dad. To be a good son and do a big right, I had to be a bad son and do a little wrong. The universe remained tilted to the positive. Condemn me if you must. Send me to perdition and damnation with or without a hug. The greater good has been done.

———

"Where are you and Dad going?" she insisted. Mom had her hands on her hips, a sure sign of inflexibility. She had asked several times over the last few days, her maternal radar sensing something out of kilter. I had to give a little rope.

I lived and worked in Alexandria, Virginia, helping government agencies untangle their agendas, plan their futures, and get the best use of technology. Every year or two, I left my office and home, jetted cross-country to pick up Dad in Elko, and ushered him off to a favorite fishing hole or a scenic getaway, usually some locale attainable only by plane or a slow trot by jeep. Mom knew of these excursions and harbored a subtle suspicion about them, but I valued every one of them, viewing each as an exclusive father-son getaway. The less people knew of our shenanigans, the better.

"If you must know," I would tell her while walking away, "we are flying to Washington and going from there." I chose each word carefully. Then I would hurry outside.

Here the deception found life. From my inner ear came Sister Mary Kathleen's ghostly German voice—"A partial truth is a whole lie." Sister Dennis appeared next to her, nodding.

Mom and everyone I told expected Dad and me to fly into Washington State and drive from there through Canada to Alaska. Two years before, he and I had flown to Anchorage, fished for halibut and salmon, cruised the glaciers, and landed a Cessna atop Mount McKinley. Dad had caught a sixty-eight-pound halibut, the second largest of the day, among men half his age and received a trophy photo. He still raved about the experience, so naturally everyone expected me to plan a similar trip this time.

The deception cleverly gave me license to get Dad's passport from Mom. She asked, "Why do you need that?"

I replied, "Where do you think we're going?"

"To Alaska."

"And how do you think we would get there?"

"Through Canada."

"Which is what?"

"A different country."

"Does that answer your question?"

"I guess so." She sent the passport within a week.

The whole truth was that *Washington* meant *Washington, DC.* The rest of the statement, ". . . and going from there," was equally ambiguous since understanding it depended on accurately interpreting what preceded it. I relied on an old truism that precise answers depended on precise questions, a burden shared equally by the questioner and the questioned. By contrast, vague questions produced vague answers. I saw Sister Mary Kathleen and Sister Dennis rolling their eyes and frowning at my alleged loophole.

This deception was born of frustration. For more than ten years, the family had considered a trip to Spain for Dad's sake. That's how it started—*for Dad's sake.* Discussion came as loose chatter in phone calls and e-mail without coalescing into a coherent plan.

During Thanksgiving and Christmas dinners, the conversation intensified, with everyone agreeing the idea had merit but no one showing the wherewithal to see it through, much like Middle East peace. Every year, the banter followed more or less the same pattern.

"We should go to Spain." Jonna, my older sister, typically initiated the dialogue. It gave her a feeling of control.

"I don' want to go." Dad feigned immediate disinterest.

"Where would we go?" Amy, my younger sister, chimed in.

"We should all go," Mom warmly added, "and Aunt Anita might want to come too, and Uncle John. You can't leave them out."

"If we go, I don't want to stay just in Spain." Amy's worldliness showed.

"We'll need more than one car." Jonna began her logistics.

"Do they have French fries?" asked little Alexis, my niece, pressing two fingers into her mashed potatoes.

"Of course they do, dork!" Jacob retorted, as brothers do.

"We'll have to see the whole family," intoned Mom. "I want to see my mom's family too, not just Dad's."

About then, Roger, my brother-in-law, went outside for a cigarette.

"How long would we stay?" Jonna continued plotting without interruption.

"Maybe I can meet you somewhere," Amy volunteered, sipping red wine. "I might go to other countries in Europe."

"Not by yourself, you're not," scolded Mom, in full protective mode.

"I don' want to go," Dad repeated, again feigning disinterest.

"Do they have catsup?"

"Where would we fly into?"

"I'd like to see southern Spain too."

"Who else might want to come?"

And the roles continued for an hour until I raised my own voice—"Mom, your turkey is juicy and delicious." Everyone around the table agreed, which launched Mom into a soliloquy of exact temperature, time, butter rub, and basting. The Spain discussion ended.

These chaotic minutes resembled the planning of a traveling circus—old people and small children, a caravan of multiple cars, competing interests and agendas, sibling rivalries, French fries, a little smoke, flying monkeys, and cotton candy. The trip became a Frankenstein and sounded, as each minute passed, less for Dad's sake.

Dad had turned seventy-eight years old in September 2008. He needed two naps a day and close proximity to a bathroom to avoid issues. After his bypass surgery and hip replacement, he couldn't walk long distances and his sense of direction had turned upside down—left had become right and vice versa. He needed more than ten pills a day, some in the morning, some at night, to regulate his heart, control diabetes, and thin his blood.

Over the previous five years, he and I had vacationed in Alaska, Yellowstone, and Glacier. I had tended to him one-on-one and we had managed well together, though not without difficulty. Now, picturing an entourage of family and friends, small children and multiple cars, I imagined how infinitely complex it would be to tend to his needs and how miserable he would become in the process.

The chance for a family trip diminished as each Thanksgiving and Christmas passed. Dad's age and health (not to mention Mom's) crept into the dinner dialogue, subtly at first, with whispers and wide-eyed glances, and later more boldly as someone asked, "Is Dad well enough to go?"

Still, the family remained paralyzed by the traveling circus and no concrete decisions were ever made. By the time I moved the conversation on to the juiciness of Mom's turkey, we had tacitly agreed to shelve Spain for another year, knowing that postponement doomed the plan.

The sole question for me—Did Dad *need* to make the trip? I talked with my cousin Amaia in Mondragón, Spain. Educated in London, she spoke English fluently, worked for a shipping company, and seemed the most worldly of all our cousins. She told me that Dad's twin, Anita, had been diagnosed with Alzheimer's and placed in a nursing home in Lekeitio. Her condition had worsened each day. Another sister, Juanita, stayed at the same nursing home, having suffered a stroke two years earlier. Would these sisters survive another year, another five years? Who could say, but it became increasingly unlikely.

Dad needed to see his sisters. That's where I came down on the matter. I knew this because I would need to see my sisters—Jonna and Amy—if the two of them, in their doddering old age, sat side by side in a nursing home. I would chew glass to see them one last time, hug them, hold their hands, and help them remember those precious moments of childhood that sparked happiness and joy. In our few years on this planet, as cosmic lint in a vast universe, nothing rivaled a shared bloodline. After hanging up with Cousin Amaia, I resolved to take Dad to Spain on my own.

There would be consequences for whisking him away. Mom, Jonna, and Amy—three stubborn, opinionated women whom God Almighty saw fit to perch in my family tree—would simmer until their anger boiled over into rants and howls of injustice. For the rest of my life I would hear about my treachery and wickedness. The stain would never be washed away. The story would be interred in the pantheon of told and retold stories at every family event. I knew and expected this. All sin—even confessed sin—bore its own punishment.

Still, I needed a counterbalance to mitigate an all-out bloodletting. I gave Mom, her sister, Anita, and her two sisters-in-law, Mabyn and Mary Lou, a Christmas gift to the Cherry Blossom Festival in Washington, DC, that would coincide with my secret trip with Dad. I put them up in a swanky hotel in Old Town Alexandria, ordered matching sweatshirts, and arranged for a few events. Amy came down from New York to meet them. If Mom and Amy fumed, they would have to rant and cuss while enjoying the aromatic fragrances surrounding the Jefferson Memorial. In the meantime, Jonna, Roger, and my niece and nephew would travel to Hawaii.

Here again I benefited from a lesson that the good Catholic sisters of my youth had taught me. Guilt, when properly applied, could subdue fury. These sacrificial offerings would blunt the anger, not eliminate it, but some eternal relief was better than none at all.

———— ∞ ————

Dad knew nothing of our true destination as we drove from Elko to Salt Lake City. I reinforced the deception by restating it—*flying to Washington and going from there.* Of everyone in the family, Dad grasped geography least, which surprisingly prompted him to ask, "Washington State or Washington, DC?" I ignored the query and pointed out the weather conditions, a subject that offered him unending fascination.

In Washington, DC, we stayed overnight at my condo. Having now abandoned the idea of Alaska, he thought we'd leave for Canada and fish somewhere in Quebec. I neither confirmed nor denied his expectations.

His inquisitiveness peaked the next day at the Dulles ticket counter. He leaned close to the frazzled woman looking over our passports.

"Where we goin'?" he asked.

"Looks like you're going to Bilbao, Spain," she said.

"What?"

"Bilbao, Spain."

Dad looked at me. I raised my eyebrows and smiled. "Surprise."

He turned back to her.

"No, no, come on, where we goin'?"

"Sir," she said emphatically, "you have two first-class tickets to Bilbao, Spain."

"You one crazy woman," he said. "Dat no right."

"It is, sir."

Dad tossed up his hands. "Well, I not goin'. I goin' walking home."

"The door's over there, Dad, and it's a long, long walk home. Don't get hit by a car. There's six lanes." I had learned years before to call Dad's bluffs.

After our security check, he raised a finger at me. "You tell me now. Where we goin'?"

"Dad, the lady told you. We're going to Bilbao."

As we crossed the Atlantic, a trip that Dad had first made more than sixty years before, I thought about how this journey, probably his last, compared with his first. Six decades earlier, he had come to America in a military transport, over a span of twenty days, leapfrogging from city to city for fuel, no amenities, no food, no warmth, the rumble of four mammoth engines ringing in his ears. Young and energetic, he had contorted himself into tight quarters, slept upright, held his bladder, and vibrated for hours in rhythm with the fuselage. Hope and a heel of bread had kept him nourished. Leaving the doldrums of Franco's Spain to explore a new world, he had felt a wellspring of idealism and a yearning for a land of plenty, work, and opportunity. He had left everything for America and arriving with nothing, he had built everything.

Now he was returning an old man. In first class, he was served Caesar salad, smoked salmon, grilled mahimahi, chocolate cheesecake, and fine wines. The silverware was chilled. Instead of a heel, he had a choice of white, wheat, or rye bread, warmed and topped with melted butter. Heated cloths were brought with tongs to clean our hands and face. After he ate, he sorted out seven pills and gulped them down with Perrier. He had a selection of two hundred movies and a thousand songs on his own television console, and his seat reclined to become a bed, a luxury he indulged with a fat pillow and a thick blanket.

As he slept, my eyes traced the lines of his face. I thought about life's balance. In youth, so ebullient and free, we craved luxuries, but once we acquired them, our ebullience waned and with it, youth. Nature demanded trade-offs, balance. It was inescapable and cruel.

In Frankfurt, Germany, having landed late, we raced to our next gate.

"Where we goin'?"

"Dad, we're already in Europe. Where did I tell you? Let me carry your bag." Extra weight caused pain on his hip.

"No, I carry it."

"I can carry it until we get to the gate, and then you can have it back."

"No, dis mine. I carry it. You don't dink I can?"

"I didn't say you couldn't. Just get a move on."

I discovered one of his tells, secret signs that revealed something important about his thoughts, that he probably didn't know he had. Older people fear losing independence when children assume power of attorney and control of bank accounts, bill paying, and other functions of living. But after everything material gets stripped away, they still cling to one or two small functions that serve as receptacles of continued power and independence over their lives—planting flowers in the garden, taking out the trash, waxing the car, sewing buttons on, or fixing a faucet. The activity becomes a symbolic declaration that they have power, control, and independence. Removing the symbolic with the material eliminates any reason for living.

In Dad's case, carrying a suitcase showed that he was an independent man with power and control over his own actions. I let him carry it, and let him still, and push back others who want to carry it for him. Dignity comes in many currencies.

On our plane to Bilbao, Dad glued his eyes on the window for ninety minutes.

"Where we goin'?" he asked again, and would ask twice more en route.

"Bilbao, Spain," I responded each time, thumbing through a magazine.

He didn't believe in the destination, yet frantically searched for it. Why the contradiction? I thought maybe because the trip had exceeded the limits of his imagination.

A few days before, he had been lounging in his La-Z-Boy and flipping channels on the remote. He waited to take his pills and eat to settle the medicine and then reclined for a nap. Out in the yard, he had work to do, but it could wait another day. He had to walk Chata, our dog, but she could wait too until after lunch.

Nowhere in this daily routine had he dreamt of boarding a plane, crossing an ocean, and walking again on Basque soil, breathing salt air, seeing his sisters and brother now twenty years older, or visiting those childhood places seared in his mind—in all our minds. When his dreams shrank, so did his faith in the impossible.

The plane made its final descent. Peering through the little window, he remained unconvinced.

"What place dis?"

"Bilbao, Spain."

I recognized then the power of sensations. Only part of him believed what he had been told. The part that searched longingly for a glimpse of his birth country was the part that trusted me, his son, implicitly. The other part could not accept where he was until sensations washed over him.

He needed to see Euskadi, its wetness and greenery, smell the salt and grime of Bilbao, feel the humid air, and hear the guttural tones of Basque jargon on every street corner. Those bombardments would shake loose his imagination and hopefully inflate earthbound dreams in desperate need of lightness and air.

On the drive from the airport to our secluded hotel, the Palacio Urgoiti atop a hill overlooking Mungia and a short distance from the heart of Bilbao, he studied the thick foliage of pine, elm, oak, and tall grasses, a smattering of

tulip and daisy and what looked like bluebonnets and marigolds, small sun-
flowers, purple orchids, and twisted vines from dense jungle.

A light rain tapped at our windshield.

He turned to me and muttered, "We in Spain."

A smile widened his face.

"Yes, Dad, we are."

## 2

"Put the light here." Dad pointed. Placenta oozed off his hand.

I moved the beam as frost floated in the light. My hands and legs shook
through my thin pajamas, coat, and stocking cap.

In a bed of straw, a ewe lay on her side, stomach bloated, heaving up and
down in painful rapid rhythm. Plumes of warm air billowed from her snout
like a steam engine. Her long ears drooped around a black face, and glassy
eyes, dull and empty, teetered closer to death than life.

When she bleated, her neck craned back and out squeezed a dry, cracking
voice. Across her belly where Dad had wiped his hands, streaks of red and pink
stained the wool, and in the beam the blood looked more black than red.

Two hours past midnight, the barn was twenty degrees warmer than the
February air outside. Darkness and stillness surrounded us. The trough had
frozen over. No water. The other ewes bunched on one side to stay warm and
give privacy to their sister ewe. A seven-year-old ascribed such courtesies to
sheep and cows, even trees and rocks.

Dad knelt in the straw behind the ewe, his hot breath visible in the light,
puffing at half the sheep's pace.

By his feet sprawled a lamb—bony-legged with oversized hooves, eyes
closed, maybe six pounds, unmoving, un-breathing. The tongue dangled to the
side.

I stared at the little thing. Dad had partially covered its head with straw,
but I could see the contorted face, the hanging tongue, the short agony, the
permanent death. My seven-year-old mind took the image and stored it up,
allowing me to recall it with immediate clarity through life.

My light wandered as I studied the baby carcass.

"Put the light here," Dad said again with urgency.

Sweat rolled down his cheeks and steam curled from his balding scalp. He reached at my hand and moved the light to the right spot. Blood touched my skin and I squirmed.

Lifting the ewe's hind leg, he eased his hand into her birthing canal. She groaned as the cervix widened around his burly forearm. Her glassy eyes dulled as spirit drained.

"Leppie, come on, Leppie," Dad whispered in the quiet.

He pushed in up to the elbow and with his other hand pressed on her belly. A strained, painful high-toned whimper came from her dry throat.

"Come on, Leppie," Dad half spoke, half hissed.

My light fixed on the elbow. Anxiety made me warm and I did not blink.

His arm came out. Pinched between two fingers, surrounded in red syrup, he had hold of a wet ear. Pulling gently, he coaxed out a black stubble crown, then a nose and neck, one leg, a second leg, then all four. The placenta ejected into the straw.

My light followed the lamb out. It lay still in the straw.

After wiping his hand and arm on the ewe's wool, he punctured the thin sack around the lamb's face. Fluid spilled out. He hooked his finger in the small mouth and scooped out gunk.

Still no movement.

He cleaned a finger on his pants and reached in a second time.

The ewes at the end of the barn stopped chewing their cud and a cathedral quiet fell as a heavy pall.

Dad blew in its mouth and the lamb's long tail twitched and wiggled like a starter switch. There in the straw lay new life. I took a breath.

The weakest, smallest bleat broke the cold darkness. The newborn had found its voice in the world. The little creature's mother meekly raised her head and cracked a pitiful whimper of welcome before plopping down.

After her, the ewes across the way sounded off, one after the other, as a happy chorus. Those who understand sheep best have good reason to declare them among the most unintelligent beasts on the planet. But on this evening, I considered such judgment to be incomplete or inaccurate as I listened to the ewes moderating their voices depending on the mood of the barn—chewing their cud in wait, remaining still at the moment of birth, or bleating loudly after the herd increased by one. There was joy in this February frost.

Dad held a vial of penicillin in the circle of my flashlight, filled a syringe, and injected the ewe's thigh. He cleared away the placental mulch and packed new dry straw around her head and belly. My light wandered back and forth between the dead lamb at his feet and the newborn that tried to stand on four knobby, furry toothpicks before falling and trying again.

Picking up the living twin, who shook with cold and fright, he gently zipped her little body inside his vest until the head stuck out at his neckline. He grabbed the dead twin by the two hind legs, letting the head dangle a couple of inches from the ground. The tongue stuck out, frozen against the toothless gums.

"Let's go to bed," he said.

We left the barn. I walked a few feet behind, focusing the light on the swinging head and flopping ears of the dead lamb. I worried it might hit the ground. At age seven, I had not been acquainted with death.

As we passed Dad's blue pickup, he tossed the dead lamb into the truck's bed. There its mangled features and wrinkled skin recorded the last moment of life.

Inside the house, he cut five holes in a grain bag—one for the head, four for the legs—and swaddled the living lamb in a burlap sweater, placing her in a cardboard box cushioned with a pillow and leaving her in our laundry room for the night.

I turned off my flashlight, which was now stained with blood. In my room, down a short hallway from the laundry, I fell asleep to the weak, warm voice of the living lamb. The dead lamb visited my dreams.

———

"Damn it, Joe, did you take him out last night?" With hand on hip, Mom clutched a dish towel with the other as we sat for breakfast. A washrag, slung over her shoulder or squeezed in her fist, crept into every image that I had of her.

"He got to learn," Dad replied.

He sat on a barstool at the end of the counter, inhaling slowly from a cigarette that burned orange at the tip. Smoke rose and hung near the ceiling.

Mom served oatmeal or Cream of Wheat for my sister and me, while making egg salad or peanut butter and jelly sandwiches for our lunches. By the time she sealed the latches on our pails, we had to swallow our last bite of breakfast. Mom had a schedule and first grade started in thirty minutes.

Dad often used the phrase "He got to learn." Though nonspecific and always after the fact, it usually rebuffed Mom's overprotective nature. I wondered what I was supposed to learn and if I had successfully learned it.

Filled with doubt, I pondered everything. I felt that if I thought long enough, the wisdom would come, and if it didn't, then I was either not meant to have it or I wasn't smart enough to know it. The two weeks caring for the living lamb gave me a chance to learn, though learn what remained elusive.

Before school each morning, Dad scooped white powder into a fat green bottle and filled it with warm water. Pressing his thumb over the neck, he shook the contents and stretched a black rubber nipple at the end.

"What is that?" I watched him cut a cross at the nipple's tip with his ivory-handled pocketknife.

"Milk," he said.

"Can I taste it?"

"You won't like it."

"Why not?"

" 'Cause you no lamb."

"Let me try."

He dabbed several drops into my palm and I licked it like a cat from a saucer. I gagged, wiping the rest on my pants and scraping my tongue to rub out the chalky, iron taste. Dad laughed.

The living lamb struggled with the nipple, but it learned to suck quickly. Its tail wiggled like a Richter needle. I counted each of the ribs under its dried gray fur, touching its nose as milk frothed, and thinking to catch the bouncing tail, but opting instead not to disrupt what seemed to be a wiggling barometer of happiness.

"What happened to the other lamb?" I asked.

"What oder lamb?"

"The one in the pickup." I paused, thinking that I had dreamt the contorted face and the dangling head.

"It's dead," he said. "I take it to de dump today."

The answer seemed hard and mean. He looked at me, at the lamb, then me again. His forehead wrinkled and his bushy brows merged into one. The lamb continued its joyful frothing.

"It don' matter. Dat's his time. God, He sit up dere."

He took his hand from the nipple and pointed up.

"He got one big book. And He look in it every day and He move His finger down de book and He say, 'Whose time today? Who comin' up here? Who goin' down dere?' and if He see your name dere, it don' matter who you are, it your time. Don' matter if you rich or got one big house or if you de president of de Uni'ed Stets. When it your time, it your time. It de lamb's time. Dat's all."

"Is my name in the book?"

"Yes. Mine too. And your mama's and your sister's. Everybody in de book. It don' matter."

"Is it a long time away?"

"What a long time away?"

"When your name comes up."

He seemed bothered by the question, realizing perhaps that he wasn't prepared to answer it.

"You don' know. Nobody know. Maybe today, maybe tomorrow, maybe hundred years."

"So you could be in the book for tomorrow?"

Dad hummed as the lamb closed its eyes, nursed and gurgled.

"No," Dad said.

"But if no one knows, how do you know?"

"I got lots of work to do."

"I don't understand."

"I just know."

"And are Mom and Jonna in the book?"

"Yes."

"When are they in the book?"

"Not for one long time."

"How do you know?"

" 'Cause I know. We not in de book for one long time."

"But how do you know I'm not in the book for today or tomorrow?"

"I know." He raised his voice emphatically. "You got feeling 'bout dose things." He moved his hand from the lamb's nose and tapped his chest with two fingers.

The living lamb's belly puffed out. It wanted more and would have gladly eaten until its bitty belly burst had Dad let it. Sheep knew nothing of moderation.

By then, Mom called me for school.

For seven years I had not thought about life ending, not Dad's or Mom's or Jonna's, and certainly not my own. But in a minute, Dad had changed my reality. He had put parameters around life, not for me alone but for my whole family, for the dead lamb, for the living lamb, for everyone on the planet. This new, extraordinary knowledge until then had escaped my understanding. How had something this momentous not registered with me?

This lightning defined what Dad had meant by "He got to learn." I viewed it as a conveyance of knowledge, a type of human hazing. All people—Mom and

Jonna and my classmates in first grade—had learned this universal lesson in their own time and in their own way, I thought, but each one had sworn an oath of cosmic secrecy allowing other humans to discover the truth on their own. Now I had.

I accepted the lesson with gusto. The book listed everyone's name; it had to be a thick book. It included my name too; I wondered where. It listed dates and times; I pondered tomorrow and next week, and hoped to reach Christmas and my next birthday. No one knew his time; but Dad had a "feelin' 'bout dose things."

Dad's lesson reinforced itself on our small farm. After that first night in the barn, other lambs died, and in some cases their mothers died too. Their names came up. Our sheepdog, Lady, birthed a litter of seven puppies, but two of them, born with no eyes or mouth, died within seconds outside the womb. It was their time. I found magpies teeming with maggots in the field. It was their time. A long-tailed rat lay on its side by the trough in the barn. Its name had come up.

We received a phone call from Dad's twin sister, Anita, in Spain. She said that Grandma had died. Amuma, eighty-six years old, gray-haired, and stocky, had raised eight children, worked, cooked and cleaned, and cut her own wood for a rustic stove. The phone call lasted less than ten minutes. I didn't know how to feel when Dad shared the news. I watched him for cues—a few tears, hands over his face, a need to be alone. But he showed nothing. I imagined he said, "It was her time." I felt more certain than ever of the life lesson.

Dad's formula offered simplicity and made sense to me. Without God's Book of Names, I couldn't process death for lambs or people. Without the structure, a life of blubbering followed whenever family, friends, or little lambs met their maker.

Unfortunately, life offered nothing so clean as Dad's simple formula. We had a sleek white cat on the farm that Mom had named, appropriately, Momma Cat. Mom named all the animals after their habits or lifestyles, much like Dickens named his characters after their determined role in a novel. Momma Cat had a strikingly long tail, a narrow back, one yellow eye, one blue eye, and a peaceful, cuddly demeanor that masked a patient skill as a hypnotic huntress.

I enjoyed watching her work. She sat in the center of our front lawn and waited for magpies to perch on a low-hanging power line. She remained totally still, blending her white short hair into tranquil, quiet surroundings.

Eventually, a naive magpie dropped from the line to the lawn, bobbed its black head, looked around, and cawed obnoxiously. It stayed in one place and so did Momma Cat. It hopped an inch closer and she patiently lay in the grass. Another inch it came and still she remained a granite statue. Then within a foot, eye to eye, and peaceful, cuddly Momma Cat leapt from her spot with the agility of a lion, extending a single paw with sharpened claws to snag a wing or leg or head. Rarely did the magpie escape.

Word never got around the magpie community that our front lawn had become a treacherous place for their kind. Momma Cat lured a magpie once a week, but she didn't eat them. She enjoyed the hunt. It was their time.

Mom did not name her Momma Cat for her hunting skills. Even by cat standards, Momma Cat was a promiscuous seductress, creating a new litter of kitties every twelve to sixteen months. We usually gave away her kittens by their sixth week, so many of the households and ranches surrounding our farm in Elko became beneficiaries of Momma Cat's progeny.

We kept one of her kittens, a white and gray male, to reduce mice and rats in the barn. Mom named him Tom. He fought constantly with other cats and even provoked our sheepdog, Lady, into mortal combat. Part Australian dingo, Lady stood four times his size, yet Tom held his own with spit and hiss, an arched back, elongated claws, and a cougar's growl. With a torn ear and a broken tail, he had a record of fighting to the end even if he pushed only to a standoff, as he often did with Lady. Dad said he was part rattlesnake. Tom played with and tormented the mice and birds he caught in the barn, crippling them with a bite and batting them back and forth before growling and crunching down on their heads. Other cats deposited their trophies on our doorstep. Tom ate his.

Even at a year old, Tom continued nursing on Momma Cat. Bigger and stronger than she was, he held her down and tore her up, moving from one tit to another and drying up her milk. Mom would smack him with a broom, which made him mad, and he raised his back to an arch and stood his hair on end and ripped bristles from the broom before Mom successfully shooed him back to the barn and brought Momma Cat in the house to nurse her wounds. Tom scared me.

Right on schedule, Momma Cat got pregnant again and gave birth a couple of months later to a litter of six kittens. All six lived. It was not their time. Mom put a blanket in a box much like Dad had done for the living lamb, and we admired their pink noses, closed eyes, perfectly formed paws. Instantly, they knew how to suckle and draw milk. Mom checked on them through the day, and at night we put the box in the garage out of the cold.

A couple weeks later, when I checked on the kittens before school, a startling macabre sight met my eyes and a sudden jolt froze my muscles, like electricity through water. I yelled for Mom, who then covered my eyes, ordered me to the house, and called for Dad.

Banging, yelling, cussing, flying objects—sounds of battle ensued, gladiators all, Daniel in the lions' den. When the crashing stopped, Dad came out of the garage carrying a grain sack tied at the top with baling wire. It jostled and raged like caged scorpions and out of it snarled growls and hisses and screeches of bloodlust.

Tom was inside. I had seen a glimpse of his nefarious handiwork. He had returned in the night to nurse on Momma Cat, but found there in his traditional place six newly born kittens tugging at her six tits. Jealousy had overcome him and he had chewed off their heads and torn off their limbs. Little spatters of blood stained the cement floor—scatterings of furry little heads with closed eyes, a tail here, a leg there—death all around.

Mom called Tom a "son of a bitch" and made Dad take him to one of the big ranches in Ruby Valley or Lamoille. A few months later I learned that among hundreds of other cats, Tom had become enamored of a feline whose blood coursed with bobcat. He met a violent end.

The scene in the garage haunted me for weeks. I thought about it all the time—in school, at home reading, when eating dinner. It trespassed in my dreams. It made me think of the fragility of kittens and by extension the fragility of humans and how disorderly the whole apparatus of life was from beginning to end.

When I learned to tie my shoes, my laces always undid themselves, prompting Mom to scold and say, "Tie your shoes before you trip," and yet when I wanted them untied before bed or when a game on the living room floor required them to be taken hurriedly off my feet, they always seemed impenetrably knotted. A profound nonsense plagued the world, ups when I wanted downs and downs when I wanted ups. I wondered how a divine inspiration could be so topsy-turvy.

"Were the kittens in God's Book?" I asked Dad.

"Yes, prob'ly," he replied.

"So God wanted Tom to kill them?"

"No. Tom's one rattlesnake."

"So God didn't want the kitties to die?"

"Dere's nothin' He don' know. But you got to find out on your own."

He clicked his tongue to show impatience.

"I got work. I need your help. You come."

As I grew older, I uncovered a common pattern in our conversations. I asked questions and Dad answered several. After a few, he realized how much work he had to do and he needed my help to do it. Idle hands were the devil's playground, and apparently, so too were questions.

Nonetheless, our short dialogues offered a kind of condensed reflection. Had they been any longer, I might have forgotten all or part of them. Had they been any shorter, they would have been less meaningful. Their succinctness offered an idea that I pondered and wrestled with until I settled on my own peculiar understanding of what Dad wanted me to learn.

God's Book of Names I figured was not an absolute record. But if it was God's Book, how could it have limitations? This conundrum stumped me for weeks. It meant that either Dad was wrong or God was. Neither conclusion suited me. In fact, both thoughts received no more consideration than if my first-grade teacher had told me that two and two made five. Saying it out loud did not make it a viable option. A child's mind had a way of making everything possible and impossible at the same time. Ideas crept in as seeds on fertile soil. There had to be another explanation, the correct explanation, one that rendered four as the sum of two and two.

Once I stumbled on it, the answer seemed obvious. God's Book was not a record of when or how everyone and everything died, but rather a record of when or how everyone and everything died—*naturally*. Dad was right and so was God. If someone or something lived life as God intended, then the record was exact—chapter, page, line, and letter—a paragon of perfection.

No one knew what God intended, not even Dad. He would be the first to admit that. More profound, no one knew the meaning of a natural or unnatural act—only God did. But humans were too small and pitiful to comprehend the real difference between the two or to understand what God truly wanted from each of us.

God's Book remained simultaneously precise, unknowable, and infinite in scope. Dad acknowledged this when he said, "Dere's nothin' He don' know." Our task remained glimpsing His infinite knowledge; in Dad's words, "But you got to find out on your own."

What should I do? How should I act? A divinity shaped our end, but what about all the steps leading up to our end, the in-between time? I agonized over this puzzle and settled on one thing. What happened between birth and death was up to me, Dad, Mom, Jonna—all of us.

This realization frightened me. Until then, I had taken comfort knowing that God's Book determined when I died no matter what I did or didn't do in life. In short, I didn't need to be responsible for my conduct. To be young and carefree was very heaven. What would be would be. All deviations had been planned, all decisions considered. Spontaneity was an illusion. That was pre-Tom.

My post-Tom world shifted the heaviest weight—life itself—from God's broad shoulders to mine. Early one morning, I was a child with an unknown, yet absolutely pre-defined purpose; a week later, a blank slate, bumping around in the cosmos with a unique conscience and no destiny. I put away childish things. That I would live was up to God. How I would live was up to me.

As a Catholic, Dad shared this sentiment. He went to church for funerals, weddings, or the occasional baptism, but he did not put cash in the priest's plate, attend Sunday Mass, say the Rosary, render confession, or pray conventional prayers. He knelt only to mend irrigation hoses in the field. Despite not paying homage to these rituals, he sought God's intentions through daily deeds and hard work to find out for himself what he had to learn.

Not to mislead, Dad did not wake each morning saying, "Today I will discover God's intentions." The thought did not cross his mind. Instead, he simply lived, sat in wonder of small things, and labored honestly. Wonderment and joy showed his prayerful worship.

Many times I thought about the origins of his unspoken devotion. I came up with no single or complete answer. What I found instead was a multitudinous mess of threads that gave less than a snippet of his life, but each one led to the next, then the next. Some repelled one another; others braided together, entwined, and crisscrossed until out of the knots and twists emerged a kind of clarity, like random colors in a kaleidoscope coalescing into orderly designs and unexpected patterns.

If the Divine expected us to learn about His ways, ordaining our destination but not our journey, then Dad's utterance "He got to learn" was a commandment born of heaven to be fulfilled here on earth.

# 3

I awoke in Mungia's Palacio Urgoiti to Dad blowing his nose. To say "blowing his nose" mistook a fire hydrant for a garden hose. Every morning for eighteen years, I had woken with such regularity to his explosive olfactory horn that my biological clock had molded to it and now I wake each morning at the same time as my mind conjures his kerchief and replays his percussive sound. If ever he fell ill, constant rumbling like ships docking in Boston Harbor shook the house through the night.

He paced nervously in his underwear. With trembling hands, he pulled shirts and pants from his suitcase, mixing and matching, trying to create a proper ensemble. Jet lag from our nine hours of flight hadn't affected him.

With a thin wardrobe of denim and polos, and dutiful attention from Mom, who had laid out his clothes every morning for over forty years, he ordinarily had little to worry about. When he was left on his own, however, fashion sense went adrift—mismatched socks, backward T-shirts, holey underwear—but no combination derailed completely, as Dad owned only solids, never stripes or plaids, and if an outfit neared disaster status, he simply pulled on a sweater to hide the mess underneath.

There were exceptions. One time when he had come in from the sheep barn, baling wire from the haystack was knotted in two places around his midsection, holding his pants in place.

"Dad, what's that around your waist?"

"Belt," he said, and then returned to the barn.

Lying in bed, I watched him struggle and cuss. Though he was nearing eighty, his back showed defined muscle, firm and strong, from so many years of hard labor lifting and moving and carrying and pushing. Without his false teeth, his words became mumbles, but his tone and manner expressed a frustration welling up.

"What's wrong?" I asked him.

"Got to fin' somedin' nice. Can't look like one bum."

"Calm down. Let me help you."

I got up and found Levi's and a sweater. "What about this?"

"No, I try dat. It look like one pile of shit."

"Okay, what about this?" I offered a different pair of Levi's and a nearly identical shirt.

"Dat's no good."

From my suitcase, I pulled out a red polo and a patterned sweater. Standing in front of the mirror, he pulled them over his head. I folded the collar over the neck. The dullness brightened and the mirror threw back a toothless smile.

"You don't look like a bum now," I said.

"I'm one old man." He stared as though he and his reflection had not been properly acquainted.

"We all get old, Dad."

"What Amaia say?" He changed the subject.

"We'll see Tía Anita and Tía Juanita at the nursing home in Lekeitio." I had to adjust my vocabulary while in Spain, using the Spanish *tía* for *aunt* and *tío* for *uncle*.

"Amaia be dere?"

"Yes."

"She de only one coming?"

"No, I think Amaia will bring the family."

"Everybody goin' to be dere?"

"I don't know about everybody, but quite a few."

He continued his long gaze in the mirror. I didn't know what it said. Did he worry about not being recognized after twenty years? Did he worry about appearing inadequate? Did he worry that age made him less a man, less whole in some way? Or as he studied his wrinkles and sagging jowls, did he wonder how he had arrived at this time and place? Did a reflection here in Euskadi make him think of his Basque youth or adulthood in America?

"What are you thinking about?" I asked him.

"Noding." He sat on the bed to pull on socks and Velcro his shoes.

The mirror had kept its secrets. So had Dad.

———

We rented a silver four-wheel-drive Subaru station wagon—automatic, not stick—with built-in GPS suctioned to the windshield. Most cars in Europe used stick. To find an automatic required special concessions from the dealer. Though wimpy with less power, it climbed the narrow winding roads of the Pyrenees without grinding gears.

"What's dat?" Dad pointed.

"They call this a GPS."

"What it do?"

"It tells us how to get anywhere in Spain, or anywhere in the world. We put the address here." I typed in Tía Anita's nursing home. "Then you press here, and it makes all the directions."

"I can't follow dat."

"You don't have to, Dad. It'll talk to us."

"Bullshit!" he blurted.

Then a warm female voice with a British accent told us to go five hundred meters and turn right.

"How dey make someding like dat?"

"Smart people out there. It makes traveling easier."

"Sometimes de best travel when you get lost."

"Not today. We have to be in Lekeitio by noon."

"I don' need no machine to get dere."

"I know, but it's backup."

"You jus' go like I tell you."

And so I did. Along the route, he told of every rock and tree, where a burro and cart had overturned or a car had skidded off the road, where a lightning bolt had scorched a field or a thatched house had once stood, and how a rain had flooded one area more than another or which crop had flourished best in the rich soil.

"I don' believe I here," he said.

"Why not?"

"One dream. You know, dis land it grown, I think."

"You think so?"

"Sure, 'course. Dis some best land in all Europe." He became excited and animated looking out the window. Giddiness came over him and his face flushed. I could nearly hear his heart pounding faster. But I didn't notice the growth, at least not since my visit to Spain twenty years before.

We arrived in Lekeitio an hour early and parked outside the nursing home where Tía Anita and Tía Juanita now lived.

We walked to a small shelter across the road, and found at its center a pole nearly fifteen feet tall with a crucifix at the top. Dad studied it—limp head crowned in thorns, extended condor arms, crossed feet nailed at the ankles.

"I been here," he said.

"When?"

"Yes, yes, I know dis place. I been here. Yes, yes, I been here."

He ignored me as his excitement built. He raised his arms and twirled around.

"I come here and sell bread. I come here on one donkey. What dis cage dey put here?" A wire mesh surrounded the crucifix at the top of the pole.

"They probably did that to protect it from vandalism."

"What you mean?"

"They did that to keep people from destroying it."

"Who do dat? I no seen dat happen ever."

"People have changed, Dad."

"Crazy."

"Some of them are."

"You see, down dat road, de soldiers, dey stand dere, and dey don't see me."

"What happened if they saw you?"

"Dey take you away. Den, good-bye, Charlie." He swiveled his head down, then up the road, and glanced at one building, then another.

Along the road on each side of the statue, leafless trees grew like gnarled centurions. He walked toward them, quickening his pace as memories flooded in.

"What's up with these trees?" I asked. They looked like bony arthritic fingers reaching up through the rain-soaked pavement, demonic appendages from the netherworld.

"Dey got no leaves."

"I see that, Dad. Why not?"

"Dey cut dem off."

"All of them?"

"Yes. Dey don' want to rake dem." My experience suggested that the Basques preferred efficiency over aesthetics in nearly all things—baling wire for belts, drab solids for a wardrobe, no leaves for trees. Elegance came from utility, not flamboyance.

"Over dere"—he pointed to a door—"I pick up empty bottles of milk on Saturday and I bring dem fulled up on Sunday."

"Where'd you get the milk?"

"De goats. Dose poor goats. We got two and dey give and give and give. Dat's how we got money to live. Dose goats, dey keep us alife."

"How old were you then?"

"Six or seven. I carry dat milk on one donkey, and pick up de bottles one day, and bring dem back de next. Sometimes dey broke and make one helluva mess. And I get in trouble for losing de milk and I don' get paid. Milk de most important thing."

We moved around a corner, up a steep hill, past taverns, bakeries, small clothing stores, and towering residential apartments. Communal living seemed big and businesses small. I stopped at an ATM at the top of the incline.

"What you doin'?"

"I need euros. I don't have any cash."

"What de hell is 'yurros'?"

"It's the new money of Europe."

"What new money? You mean pesetas?"

"No, euros. There's no more pesetas." I slid my card into the ATM, punched in a code, and waited.

"Banks, dey closed on Sunday. You no get noding today."

Out slid euros. He pushed out his lower lip.

"These machines are open twenty-four hours."

I showed him the new currency. Spain had had pesetas since 1869. Although exchange rates had fluctuated wildly against the U.S. dollar, the paper and coinage had appeared relatively the same for 130 years. Franco had stamped his face on a one-peseta coin in 1948; King Juan Carlos had etched his likeness on a nickel in 1976; and a smattering of replacements had entered circulation in the eighties. Few other alterations had occurred until the euro arrived in 1999 to replace pesetas permanently by 2002.

Dad studied the pictures on the new bills that symbolized artistic periods in European architecture—cathedral windows, gateways, and bridges—each note rendered in a different color.

He handed the euros back.

"You look surprised," I said.

"I never think Franco, he give up de peseta."

"Franco's dead, Dad. This money started in 1999."

"Dey use dis in Germ'ny?"

"They do, and France and Italy and most everywhere in Europe."

"How dey make dem all equal dat way?"

"What do you mean?"

"Germ'ny, it stronger, dat 'conomy dere."

"I imagine they balanced everything out somehow, Dad."

He scratched his head and turned up another hill on our right, again quickening his pace. I followed behind.

"Dat up dere where Momma and Daddy dey buried."

Not far from the town's church, cobblestone stairs, centuries old, led to a cemetery. As the stairs narrowed at the top, the passage darkened, with limbs and thick bushes interlacing across the path like a blocked artery and concealing the headstones beyond. Neither Poe nor Hawthorne could have dreamt a more ghostly scene.

Out of breath, "You see, dey come from de church and carry de coffin up de stairs, and de priest, he prays, and de people follow, and up dere, dey bury de dead, and den dey come back down."

"Do you want to see your parents' graves?"

"No, no I don' want dat."

"Why not?"

"Too sad."

Tapping his chest, "I got Momma and Daddy here."

Bells rang from the church behind us—Andra Mari (Basilica Assumption of Santa Maria in Spanish)—an imposing structure of gray stone, pyramidal and Gothic, that dwarfed all other homes and boats of Lekeitio. It resembled the churches of so many other towns we visited—grandiose yet functional. Each church seemed shockingly large, even in villages, as though constructed as a symbol of God's importance and less a place for common folk to pray. If He had infused all creatures, from the greatest kings and queens to the smallest ants, with His infinite glory, then nothing could be small nor rendered insignificant by an act of man. The church conveyed that sentiment to me. Only man's failing in the art of engineering prevented churches from rising ever higher to touch heaven and honor His divine countenance.

A Catholic Mass was in progress, so we did not enter, though we listened to the priest offer a sermon in Basque with Latin sprinkles to fill rhetorical holes. Outside, with our ears pressed to the door, we grazed our hands over the bronze portal that was surrounded by layers of Roman arches like a heavenly gate. Had pearl been plentiful, the door would have been white, not bronze.

Dad laid his palms against the door as though drawing something from it. His reaction reminded me of Irish people kissing the Blarney Stone, a link to a past that remained unchanged and important, even when all else built up or fell to ashes around it. The church remained a permanent thread for him, connecting youth and age, past and future, no matter the ebb and flow of politics, war, life, and death. The church was Dad's Gibraltar in the North, a familiar, reliable touchstone.

24

"You okay, Dad?"

"Oh, jus' fine."

Dropping his hands from the door, he absorbed one last look and then, restoring his quickened pace, shot off toward granite stairs that he climbed with the spryness of a younger man to a massive concrete pier. Locals weighed their catch here, gutted the fish, and sold them wrapped in newspaper. Small shops offered bread and spices, pastries and potatoes, fruits and other vegetables. A line of taverns, still smelling of beer and wine from Saturday parties, had chained doors. Hundreds of unmanned fishing boats, stacked side by side, bobbed in water that sloshed and whipped the pier. Not a soul walked the platform or lounged in the boats. The Sabbath took life and death from the scene and left a soft murmur of crashing waves against a beach in the distance and a breeze blowing cold off the water.

Dad stopped at the platform's edge to see an ocean vast and blue curving at the horizon.

"You see dat island dere?" He extended a finger to a cluster of trees crowded on a mound like a turtle's shell rising from the inlet.

"My daddy's brother, Vicente, put one herd of sheep dere. Vicente say, 'Dere's lots of grass dere.' My daddy say, 'What about de water?' and Vicente say, 'Dere's water all around.' But dis salt water, so all de sheep, dey die." Dad laughed, grimacing widely.

A sparkle through watered eyes showed happiness. His vision carried him beyond the island to waves rising and cresting. It reached north into the Atlantic, passed the edge of France, skimmed England and Iceland, and then, moving west, touched Canadian shores.

From that vantage, as had many before him, Dad witnessed his own past and the past of his people, who built wooden ships, hunted whale, fished cod, and sailed to the New World with Columbus. He saw our origins, the beginning of man, and shed salty tears like the sea from whence we came.

"So open, so free," he said.

"It is beautiful. Do you miss it?"

"No, I don', but I dream 'bout dis place." He pulled out a kerchief and blew that rumbling nose and wiped teary eyes.

"Time to get back," I told him.

"I seen nuff." He carried a lump in his throat.

At the nursing home, we came to a black iron gate among manicured hedges and pleasant grounds. I pushed the security buzzer. No answer. I called Cousin Amaia.

Soon out of the nursing home bounced Pilar, my aunt, Dad's youngest sister. Although seventy-four years old, she skipped with the spryness of a child, clutched the gate with her fists, and rattled it back and forth as if to yank it from the hinges. When it finally opened, she and Dad bear-hugged. The conversation became fast and frantic, excitement imparted through half-laughs of intoxicating surprise and joy.

Tía Pilar led us inside, where aunts, uncles, cousins, and family friends waited. No one spoke. Dad went first to Tía Juanita, who sat in a chair against the wall. Having had a stroke, she could not stand or walk and had lost both memory and speech.

"Remember me?" Dad leaned in to her.

He held her hands, looked at her intensely, willing her to recall his features. Her droopy eyes stared back with vagueness and the sagging side of her face showed no change, no recognition. Everyone waited.

Then it came. She knew! She remembered! However the mind works, one could almost see neurons and mental pathways rearranging themselves, impulses traveling down cerebral roads, taking millions of detours, and after passing through a briar patch of mental wreckage, connecting memory with recognition. An airy voice came from Tía Juanita, and the right corner of her mouth turned up in a half-smile.

Dad grabbed her head and pressed it into his chest, kissing her hair and cheeks and squeezing her in a mighty hug. With her right arm, she squeezed back while her left lazily dangled. Half the arms, half the body did not diminish the embrace. A paralysis could not subdue the heart.

Anita was already crying when Dad came to her, locked eyes, and shared a special pause.

Between those gazing eyes, a lifetime of joys and pains, happiness and despair, stretched from waking life to the womb. Could a single instance, so human, so enriched with love, exist outside normal space and time?

Whispering Basque endearments, Dad and Anita entwined in a gleeful crush, a hold of steel with eyes closed. Then a reverent silence conveyed the senti-ment—*We shall not let go, not again, never again; we shall pull this day out of time, freeze it, preserve it to recall over and over; we shall not forget it no matter age or sickness; since our parting until this day, our solemn love turned to a deep longing and then to loss, and was so deeply felt that loss turned to torture; a darkness came to our hearts, swamped our souls, and left an emptiness so bereft of hope that tears gave no comfort; if we cursed Him for our misery, we know now, on this day, that it made our sated hunger sweeter, our quenched thirst fuller, our cups runneth over; and, when we hear His calling, feel His warm light on our faces, and find our place in a loving heaven, we shall remind Him of this day and thank Him for it.*

I watched at a distance, snapped pictures, and let Dad revel in warmth. The aunts, uncles, and cousins who gathered in that small lobby pressed prayerful hands to their lips, said nothing, felt grace, and shed tears. We witnessed a perfect moment.

For the first time, I saw a thing called bliss. It is real, palpable, and rare. It arises when two hearts are connected so intricately, so lovingly that they beat as one. But tear those hearts in half, separate them by time and geography, and let them beat, bleed, and suffer alone. Body and mind feel incomplete and the soul empty. Then reunite the hearts, heal the severed halves, so they beat again as one, and in that moment, like atoms fusing, comes a brilliant force infinitely precious—a lost child returning, twins reuniting as in the womb, Christ ascending to His Father.

Here joy spoke the language of the soul. It carried people beyond age and illness, giving reprieve from the unbearable chains and pains of a clumsy world of disease and destruction.

For a sliver of time, Dad was transported up and out in the warm cuddle of Anita, and I knew that bringing about that rare splinter of light cleansed my conscience of guilt and absolved me of sin.

The Catholic sisters held no sway.

## 4

Dad remembers very little from age six. But like many of his generation, he instantly pulls out shards of memory from a single day in one of Spain's most epic struggles of the twentieth century. So many Basques, no matter their vantage in April 1936, similarly extract splinters from a single day to add fullness and truth to a violent chapter in Basque history. They hold these pieces of memory like small diamonds, never wanting the world to forget their tragedy, yet knowing that humans forget unless reminded.

Like most epic conflicts, the Spanish Civil War originated as a tug-of-war for power and a clash of ideas. In a few short months, a majority of seemingly thoughtful people conceded to the extreme left and right fringes of Spanish society. It spanned three years, hundreds of small battles, and countless deaths.

On one side of the battle stood Republicans, a loose-knit group of urban workers, peasants, some practicing Catholics, and much of the educated middle class, especially those who did not own businesses. Their coalition, dubbed leftist, became the Popular Front. Peppered among their membership were communists, Marxists, and anarchists. Volunteers from the United States, calling themselves the Abraham Lincoln Brigade, fought for the Republican cause and distinguished themselves in several skirmishes.

On the other side stood the Nationalists, a combination of military servicemen, other practicing Catholics, landowners, and many businessmen.

The Basques joined the Popular Front, not to fight necessarily for the republic but to secure assurances that if victorious, they would gain autonomy and governance over their beloved Euskadi. They risked much by the alliance but saw great rewards if they won the day. As a conservative element in the Republican coalition, like their Catalan and Galician brothers who similarly fought for autonomy, the Basques seemed out of place in the whole violent affair. Theirs was a battle within a battle.

The chief adversary of the Popular Front did not distinguish among his enemies, regardless of their motivations. Francisco Franco, a man born of a military family, led the Nationalists. Early on, he had built his military prowess in Morocco, Spain's protectorate, where a good officer received either *la caja* or *la faja* (a coffin or a general's sash). His capacity for organization and command destined him for the latter. When Spain established the General Military Academy of Zaragoza in 1928, Franco became its first director, giving him influence over the education of a new generation of army cadets and officers.

When war broke out in 1936, Franco had to choose between the Republican cause and the Nationalist coup. He chose the latter and found himself back in Morocco with authority over all Spanish forces stationed in North Africa. He was then forty-four years old and at the pinnacle of his mental faculties, talents, and social connections.

To support the coup, he had to transport thirty thousand troops from Morocco to the Iberian Peninsula. With the Spanish Navy loyal to the Republic, he reached out to Germany and Italy to secure planes and ships to move men and supplies across the Strait of Gibraltar. Both Hitler and Mussolini obliged Franco's needs, recognizing that the Spanish conflict advanced their fascist objectives, offered an experimental playground for their growing military arsenals, and cemented an alliance for any future wars on a grander scale. The maneuver succeeded. When other Spanish generals grew jealous of Franco's prominence, Hitler made it known that any support from Germany would flow only to Franco. A bond had been struck. Two months later, Franco became commander in chief, or generalissimo, of all Nationalist forces.

After a year of war, both the Popular Front and the Nationalists fought and died over mere acres. Dad recalled food shortages and every part of a household called into service—pots and pans, mattresses, wood and water. "Everyding used," he said.

The Basques proved to be fierce fighters who, according to Franco, never gave up. They did not appear to be model soldiers, though many fought brilliantly with formal regiments; they showed no military fanaticism, though some demonstrated deep talent in combat, tactics, and weaponry. Many descended from hillside homes or moved inland from seafaring ports to take up arms and fight this foe who threatened their way of life.

For them, the decision to fight arrived socially through informal conversation, toasts of wine, breaking of bread, and card games of *mus*. Their ancestors had done the same against the Romans and the Moors. They were farmers and fishermen by trade who worked with their hands, living freely and independently, men and women with gruff exteriors but gentle spirits who much preferred the quiet, solitary life to the rampages of war. Among their associations they had little hierarchy, only a dispersed command where every Basque man became a general and a soldier. They fought passionately for a personal cause, which endowed them, like other reluctant warriors, with steel spines and singular determination.

As winter 1937 melted into spring, Nationalist forces turned away from Madrid and focused on northern territories where zinc and iron mines, factories in Bilbao, and ports of commerce aided the Republican cause. By then, the Basque towns of Irun, San Sebastian, Durango, Eibar, and Bermeo had fallen. Bilbao, the proclaimed capital of Euskadi, protected itself with concentric layers of trenches and metal barricades that newspapers around the world dubbed an ingenious "Iron Ring." Still Franco's forces advanced, though at a heavy price of blood and treasure. Optimists anticipated Franco's Waterloo in the towns of Mungia and Amorebieta on the outskirts of Bilbao, where Basque opposition became ferocious and undaunted. A group of miners with strong throwing arms lit dynamite and hurled the sticks at incoming Nationalist troops. A small handful held back whole brigades for weeks.

If Basques felt optimism, Franco shared no equal measure of defeatism. In April 1937, the Nationalists eyed a small town nestled in the deep green and lush valley of the mountains nearly fifteen miles from Bilbao. Spring brought thick flowerings and carpets of grass freshly soaked with morning dew and warm rains. The town, named Guernica by Spaniards, read Gernika in deference to the Basques. It had no more than six or seven thousand people, a combination of permanent residents and a few hundred refugees who had sought safe haven in the wake of Nationalist advancements.

On Monday, Gernika's ranks swelled to ten thousand as peasants came to market from surrounding villages. The town stood between the Nationalists who marched in from the south and Bilbao that lay farther west. It had avoided the war and supported no air defenses, though it housed two army battalions as relief for Republican forces.

The Basques viewed Gernika as more than a central market. If they had had to choose, by a turn of providence, one plot of earth that defined them as a people and captured their cultural identity, Gernika would have been their selection. The Basques regarded Gernika as Catholics regard the Vatican, Jews regard Jerusalem, or Muslims regard Mecca. This hamlet pleasantly tucked away amid cathedral mountains embodied Basque history and culture, the language and religion, the people and pride of a unique and enigmatic race that had endured century after century, through conquest and withdrawal, religious upheaval and conversion, political ostracism, famine, weather, and war.

A mighty oak grew atop one of Gernika's rolling hills overlooking small homes with red clay roofs Its wide girth required three people to join hands to encircle it completely. The Basques called it Gernikako Arbola, or Tree of Gernika, and cordoned off an area around it as hallowed ground. The poet William Wordsworth, taken by the first sighting of the oak, penned a tribute to it—

> Oak of Guernica! Tree of holier power
> Than that which in Dodona did enshrine
> (So faith too fondly deemed) a voice divine
> Heard from the depths of its aerial bower—
> How canst thou flourish at this blighting hour?

What hope, what joy can sunshine bring to thee,
Or the soft breezes from the Atlantic sea,
The dews of morn, or April's tender shower?
Stroke merciful and welcome would that be
Which should extend thy branches on the ground,
If never more within their shady round
Those lofty-minded Lawgivers shall meet,
Peasant and lord, in their appointed seat,
Guardians of Biscay's ancient liberty.

Wordsworth knew that the Basques held the oak of Gernika as sacrosanct, a touchstone of liberty and a symbol of deeply rooted, permanent, and solid ancestry. Prophetically, Wordsworth's blighting hour would return during Gernika's next tender shower in April.

At the base of Gernika's oak, on this same blessed ground, the Basques had convened one of Europe's earliest general assemblies. They placed a hand upon the tree's rough bark, closed their eyes, and pledged to defend Lege Zaharra (*fueros* in Spanish), or liberties, with honor, life, and blood, vowing, "Humble before God, standing on the Basque Land." Once under oath, the men became lords of Biscay, named after the home province of Gernika.

Legend held too that Queen Isabella had knelt at the oak to promise protection of Basque *fueros* in return for allegiance to the throne, a practice that her successors often imitated to gain support from the people of Euskadi.

On one side of the oak, centuries before the U.S. House of Representatives was created, the Basques built Batzar Etxe (Casa de Juntas in Spanish), or Assembly House, to debate issues, govern daily affairs, and cast votes. Above the legislative well, ornate tapestries showed legendary Basque statesmen whose voices had once echoed from that chamber floor on days long before the European Renaissance and even earlier, before the Dark Ages of man.

On the other side of the oak and about five hundred feet down the hill, Andra Mari (Iglesia de Santa Maria in Spanish), or the Church of St. Mary, represented religion and faith. A bronze door sunken into a stone wall, similar to the one showcasing Lekeitio's church, rose into a colossal bell tower that scratched heaven.

The tree, positioned between church and state, forged the legal with the spiritual to guide the Basques in this life and prepare them for the next.

On April 26, 1937, Dad lived atop a hill in Gizaburuaga, three miles from Lekeitio and twenty-eight miles from Gernika. He saw planes fly overhead and watched them go by, "a whole sky full of dem," he said. "We seen one plane before, and we look at it 'til it go by, but we never seen dat many planes, and Daddy, he don' know what dey do, but he say, 'Dat no good,' and he was right."

By 4:30 PM, the Basques had crowded into Gernika's town square. It was Monday, market day, and peasants from Gernika and the surrounding villages had brought potatoes, wheat, beans, corn, and other vegetables and goods for sale. The market bustled with activity, high voices of bargaining and commerce. The sky reflected deep blue with wispy clouds, and the air gave scent of pine and wet grass, a reminder of Wordsworth's poetic spring rain.

Then the church bell sounded. All conversation stopped as eyes turned upward. Squinting, the people cupped their hands at their foreheads to assuage the glare—a black dot against the bright blue appeared, and then came the rumble of an engine. The marketplace scattered. People headed to shallow cellars that had been dug over the past months as Nationalist forces inched their way closer.

The plane, a twin-engine German Dornier 17, came nearer. Reducing its elevation, it unloaded twelve 50-kilogram bombs directly overhead. The church bell continued to ring, but explosions drowned it out. Then, as quickly as it had appeared, the bomber vanished.

Cautiously, the people emerged from shelters to tend the wounded and count the dead. Fires had started. A handful of bewildered citizens worked to contain the flames.

Then came, as before, black dots on blue—more than one—and bigger rumbles.

A second wave, this time Italian Savoia 79s, swooped down from the north. People huddled again into shelters thick with dust and smoke that burned their eyes and throats. The planes dropped heavier bombs. Some shelters collapsed, trapping people, who suffocated or were burned alive as fire ripped through the compartments. Others escaped and fled into the forest. The planes trailed them, dropping grenades, or strafing them with machine-gun fire.

A third attack, a fourth, and a fifth followed in quick succession. These new waves of German Junkers 52, arranged in three squadrons, carpet-bombed at twenty-minute intervals, one overlapping the next, giving little chance for civilians to find safety between drops.

The Junkers came from Hitler's Condor Legion, a special division of the Luftwaffe that experimented with aerial techniques and attack patterns to perfect the German Air Force. The Condor Legion had invented carpet bombing when it attacked Oviedo several weeks before, but that attack had not been nearly on the scale now exercised at Gernika. They dropped five-hundred-kilogram incendiary bombs, with ten times the explosive power of the earlier waves, and hundreds of anti-personnel twenty-pounders, a combination intended to raze buildings and kill civilians. The bombing lasted two and a quarter hours.

Dusk settled over Gernika as survivors climbed from shelters. It was 6:45 PM by some estimates, 7:00 PM by others. A red and orange glow lit the dimming sky. Children lay wailing under mothers who had shielded them from bullets; bodies radiated like spokes from the city center, some more than four miles away, shot in the back; cows soaked in yellow-white phosphorous and set aflame raced deliriously in circles before they smoldered and fell dead. All the buildings burned. An almshouse under the flag of the Red Cross held thirty dead orphans and two dead nuns. Shelters built to save lives trapped residents, mostly elderly, in what became mass tombs. Dotting the hillsides, lonely farmhouses burned like candles in the night. Screams punctuated the growing darkness. Survivors called the night apocalyptic, a page out of the Book of Revelation.

Noel Monks, a reporter first on the scene from the *London Daily Express,* came upon a glassy-eyed priest. "I stopped the car and went up to him," he said. "'What happened, Father?' I asked. His face was blackened, his clothes in tatters. He couldn't talk. He just pointed to the flames, then whispered: 'Aviones . . . bombas . . . mucho, mucho.'"

Bleeding and charred survivors overturned wagons and oxcarts and loaded them with random things. A line of haggard refugees with their heads hung and eyes downcast limped away from their sacred home on the path to Bilbao, a city under siege. Given the carnage of the day and the fires still blazing, there seemed nothing left of their home or the once steely spirit of an undaunted Basque people.

But that line of people came to believe in a small miracle that evening. On the hill overlooking dead bodies, burnt carcasses of cows and sheep, and heaping embers of homes, Gernikako Arbola, the great oak, remained upright and untouched, and equally unscathed by bombs stood Batzar Etxe, the People's Assembly, and Andra Mari, the church. The spiritual trio of the Basques survived, giving the people ample proof of the divine.

In the days that followed, Dad and his family hovered around a radio to listen to reports. He didn't understand the facts or the details of death, but he absorbed the raw emotion, angst, and utter despair of those close to him. His mother, strong and defiant, did not cry, though she uncharacteristically collected him up in her arms and kissed him until he couldn't breathe. His father paced the floor, wringing his hands and wondering how the people of Euskadi, how the people of the world, would react to the devastation.

Hours around the radio turned into days, then weeks. Shreds of new information about survivors, about an official Basque response, or about world reaction became small diamonds, rare and valuable. None of the news was clear at first, but a picture eventually came into focus.

More than 1,500 were killed, roughly 25 percent of Gernika's population. About 70 percent of its homes and buildings were destroyed. Since the men had been deployed to Bilbao, it was mostly women, children, and the elderly who had perished. Over the radio and in the few leaflets that made their way to Lekeitio and Gizaburuaga, Dad heard the words of José Antonio Aguirre, the designated president of Euskadi, who had taken his oath at Gernika's oak. In defiant Euskara, he showed charismatic stubbornness—

> The German airmen in the service of the Spanish rebels, have bombarded Gernika, burning the historic town which is held in such veneration by all Basques. They have sought to wound us in the most sensitive of our patriotic sentiments, once more making it entirely clear what Euskadis may expect of those who do not hesitate to destroy us down to the very sanctuary which records the centuries of our liberty and our democracy.... but victory can never be won by the invader if, raising our spirits to heights of strength and determination, we steel ourselves to his defeat.

George Steer, special correspondent for the *New York Times*, broke the story. His account ran for a week and influenced other reporters, congressional figures in the United States, and public opinion around the world. "When I entered Guernica after midnight," he reported, "houses were crashing on either side, and it was utterly impossible even for firemen to enter the centre of the town. The hospitals of Josefinas and Convento de Santa Clara were glowing heaps of embers, all the churches except that of Santa Maria were destroyed, and the few houses which still stood were doomed."

In reaction, seven U.S. senators joined the former U.S. secretary of state Henry Stimson to protest the bombing and call for a stronger embargo of a growing fascist triad from Germany, Italy, and Spain. Roosevelt declined the recommendation for fear of upsetting Catholics, who overwhelmingly supported the Vatican and Italy.

Voices in Great Britain spoke more loudly. The bombing started a slow simmer within British politics to oppose appeasement as a policy, which until then had been the focus of the Conservative prime minister, Neville Chamberlain. One year after Gernika's destruction, his policy of appeasement culminated in the signing of the Munich Agreement with Hitler to concede the Sudetenland of Czechoslovakia and laid unfortunate groundwork for the invasion in 1939 of Poland and the outbreak of World War II. The opposition Labor leader, Clement Attlee, cast the boldest stone against appeasement, declaring that aggressors naturally made demands to which men of goodwill conceded without "any guarantee that such demands would cease in the future or pave the way to any real or lasting peace."

No leader in America or Great Britain or elsewhere in the Western Hemisphere made such a lasting statement about the affairs of war and peace as Pablo Picasso, Spain's artistic savant. He had been commissioned to do a painting for the Spanish Pavilion at the Paris International Exposition, but for months he had failed to define a suitable subject for his canvas. Yet a foreboding needled his bones, and nothing in his vast creative mind had come close to capturing his pervasive darkness.

When he heard of Gernika's destruction, ideas exploded. An immediate clarity came over him. He viewed the bombing as a brutal emotional episode unparalleled in human history. Through a series of sketches, he painted in black, white, and gray shades an enormous mural called *Gernika* that depicted anguished faces stretched and wrenched in pain, horses and bulls mangled and twisted, disembodied heads floating and wandering. The mural, symbolic and allegorical, showed brutality juxtaposed with excruciating pain—war writ large.

A year after its completion, *Gernika* arrived in New York aboard the French liner *Normandie* for display at the Valentine Gallery. At the grand opening were Eleanor Roosevelt, Secretary of the Interior Harold Ickes, and other notables such as Simon Guggenheim, W. Averell Harriman, Georgia O'Keeffe, William S. Paley, and Thornton Wilder. An influential critic at the event, Elizabeth McCausland, from the *Springfield Republican,* noted in her review: "Picasso wants to cry out in horror and anguish against the invasion and destruction of the Spain of his love. He wants to protest with his art against the betrayal accomplished by Franco and his fascist allies. He wants to wake in the breasts of all who see Guernica an inner and emotional understanding of the fate of Spain. He wants simple and well-meaning citizens everywhere to live through the tragedy of bombardment, physical mutilation, and death, so that they in turn will raise their voices in a passionate cry for justice and peace."

As a sheepherder who saw artistry in sunsets and creek beds, Dad had no appreciation of cubism or other styles of modern art. Yet late in life, when he had white hair and decades between him and the events of April 1937, I showed him Picasso's painting. Left to study it, he said, "Terrible, terrible ding dat was." His impression captured Picasso's meaning and carried more value for me than the opinion of any celebrated art critic in New York, London, or Paris.

What Picasso's painting represented allegorically, Dad felt practically. Gernika became a turning point for Spain and the world. Fifteen days after the bombing, Franco pierced the Iron Ring surrounding Bilbao. The Basques still claimed to hold Plencia, Mungia, and Amorebieta, large enclaves outside the city, but optimism about victory had disappeared.

The Basques gathered nearly four thousand of their children, wrote names and vital statistics on pieces of paper, and pinned them to their jackets. Then they put the children on boats bound for England, where they arrived in May 1937, less than one month after Gernika's destruction. One twelve-year-old commented upon his arrival, "We have never tasted white bread since the war began. I have seen buildings bombed and many people killed, but never tasted white bread so good." By June 20, the Iron Ring collapsed under an unrelenting barrage from air, sea, and land. Euskadi's capital surrendered.

In a much larger sense, Gernika's destruction ushered in a new prototype for warfare. Battles no longer depended on soldiers armed with guns facing an enemy in open combat. Instead, whole cities could be bombarded in aerial assaults without the assailants knowing the difference between a true threat and an innocent civilian. This approach risked killing women, children, and the elderly. On the surface, it appeared immediately immoral in practice. But the world saw instead that bombing a town like Gernika demoralized an enemy, broke the will, and devastated the spirit. As the distance grew between the bomb that killed and the civilian who died, the immorality of taking innocent life lost its intensity and the argument lost its potency. The new age of warfare born from the ashes of Gernika later gave us the Blitzkrieg, Dresden, Hiroshima, Cambodia, and Iraq.

Nearly six decades after Gernika, a copy of Picasso's painting hung at the entry of the Security Council at the United Nations to remind us about the awfulness of war. When U.S. Secretary of State Colin Powell and CIA director George Tenet visited in 2003 to lobby for the invasion of Iraq, a sheet had been draped over the painting. The caretaker of the building said the reason was simple. No one could speak on camera without an anguished face or a wrenching horse head creeping into the picture. Picasso would have said, "That's the point." Humans forget unless reminded.

At nine years old, three years after the outbreak, Dad did not understand the consequences of Franco's victory or how it would affect him in short order. After Bilbao fell, Franco dedicated his forces and policies to stamping out Basque identity and nationalism. In the coming three decades, he would close Basque schools, forbid the teaching of the Basque language, shut down newspapers, outlaw the Basque flag, and subject Basques to ongoing search, seizure, and interrogation.

Dad's future seemed dark and inescapable. Like other Basques of his age, he proved resilient.

He had to be.

## 5

I slept the dreams of the blessed after relieving my conscience of its burden. I woke to Dad's nose blast and laughed out loud.

"Why you laugh?" Dad asked.

"Yesterday, when we were at the nursing home, I heard Tía Anita blow her nose and it sounded exactly like yours. I couldn't imagine living with both of you under one roof."

"Noding wrong with dat. She my twin."

"Nature gifted the two of you with your own personal sirens."

"You, shut up."

"Did you like seeing her?"

"Like one dream."

"I'm happy then."

"She don' 'member much."

"I could tell," I affirmed. "Amaia took my picture with her and showed it to us right after. Tía Anita looked at the picture and said, 'Who is this?' Amaia told her, 'That's you and your nephew,' and Amaia pointed at me. Then Tía Anita looked at me and twisted her eyebrows—same way you do—and she asked me, 'Who are you?' I told her I was your son and she smiled and kissed and hugged me all over again."

"Poor ding," Dad said sadly, shaking his head and stuffing his kerchief back in his pocket.

"But she remembered you, that's for sure."

"In anoder year, she won' 'member nobody."

"Probably good that we came when we did."

"Dat's right."

"You know, she remembered you after twenty years. She hasn't seen you or heard your voice or had pictures of you or anything, but somehow your face stuck in her mind better maybe than anyone else in the family."

"I her twin, dat's why."

"What it means, Dad, is if she forgets more, then your face will be one of the last things she holds on to. That's a good thing. You remember that."

"I don' know."

"Well, let's hope we don't have to find out either."

"What we doing today?"

"Going from here to Gernika and staying there the night."

"You got one room?"

"I don't."

"Dey fill up if you don' make one reservation."

"Hopefully we'll get lucky and find something."

"You won't."

"We'll take our chances."

From Bilbao, the road to Gernika snaked around wooded mountains, each mile drawing us deeper into a secluded hideaway, a Shangri-la tucked in a small valley of the Pyrenees. Overhanging oaks cast a dark, primordial shadow, almost swallowing up the whole of the road. In the open where sun touched carpets of green, old men and women worked in gardens with hoes or swept dirt paths with brooms made of tied brush. The road less traveled hadn't seen a repaving in decades, yet it had had the wherewithal to last a thousand years, like a Roman trail from Italy to France.

We dipped over the last hill to see a speck of homes and buildings carefully nestled like Easter eggs in a basket of densely radiant and emerald grass. Had the Irish seen this land, they might have returned to their island with envy in their hearts and set to work tilling the soil doubly hard to push and pull brighter colors from their tired ground, and still after so many days of plowing, they would have reached only half the splendor of Gernika's greenest of green valleys. The eye, so accustomed to dullness, had to recalibrate its spectrum to absorb the fullness of this secret realm.

"I see why this town's so important. It's beautiful," I said.

"Dat's not why dis important. Dis de place Franco, he bombed."

"I know. Seems like they recovered pretty well."

"People dey come from all 'round here for vacation or look 'round or dey come to one market dey got here. We find dat and I show you."

"Sounds good."

"If you get one room," Dad smiled with a sly tease. "Or we go back to Bilbao tonight."

"I didn't keep the room in Bilbao."

"You crazy. We goin' to sleep in de car den."

"We'll figure it out. Don't worry."

The town was lined with old buildings and narrow streets, some with original cobblestone similar to other towns in Spain, except Gernika had an uncommon cleanliness—nothing in the gutters, no trash heaps, and no foul odors of stale seawater, fish guts, or urine; no awkward placement of industrial plants or warehouses in areas rightly reserved for residences; and no blight from boarded-up buildings, broken windows, or empty lots. Natural beauty had married with rare human tidiness here.

The roofs topped in red-orange clay offered shocking contrast to the wet green of the hillsides. An artist thinking he knew all shades of green or red or orange would do well to visit this land; he would find his palette woefully inadequate to reflect its luster. The green glowed green; the red, red; the orange, orange—but as the eye danced between them, three colors turned to thirty, then three hundred, then three million, an infinite panoply of random combinations revealing every subtle gradation of light and tint, each one part real, part illusion.

I searched for a hotel near the town square.

"You not find one here," Dad reiterated, a little proud of his prediction—too proud.

I didn't respond.

A few blocks down, I spotted a hotel and spun the Subaru into the driveway.

"Do you have rooms?" I inquired of a well-groomed, broad-nosed woman with alabaster skin and hair clipped short.

"We do." She smiled. "How many?"

"Just one, two beds." I motioned for Dad to come in.

"Where you from?" she inquired warmly, hands folded on her oak desk.

"United States," Dad replied.

"Wonderful, wonderful. Your money good here!"

"Have you been busy?"

"No. I have one person. Now three." She smiled, counting the two of us.

Dad looked at me and I knew what he thought. Twenty years before, when the family had come to Spain, we had stayed in a hotel in Madrid called Gernikesa. Dad had said that his sister had worked there once and he had assured us of its marvelous reputation for being clean, accessible, and reasonably priced. But after checking in, we had become Gernikesa's first and only tenants for quite some time. The floor tilted, the windows opened to the smoke-filled kitchen on the first floor, and the sheets looked dingy, wrinkled, and twice-slept-on. Ever since, our stay there had become a running joke, and each family check-in at any hotel had prompted thoughts of Gernikesa.

When we learned that this place had only one paying customer besides us, we braced ourselves as our room door swung open. Surprisingly, the room was immaculate, with blankets and sheets turned down, a mint on the pillows, and a sweet scent of peaches.

"Dis one beautiful room," Dad acknowledged.

"And you worried we wouldn't find anything."

"I don' believe it."

We settled and then took a leisurely walk to the town center four blocks up.

"I remember that clock." I pointed as we approached. On the ground lay a clock face using hedges as numbers, but one of the hands had broken off and the other had rusted in place.

Along benches, old people bundled in coats sat admiring nothing, staring ahead. But the absences in the scene made more effect—no babies, no young people, and few boomers. In front of shops along each side road, I saw no delivery trucks or patrons coming or going. A fountain had stopped flowing, becoming instead a still pool with few coins, a poor smattering of local wishes.

"Let's go over dere. Dey got one restaurant."

"I remember. That's where Tío Joakin pushed his fork into a block of butter and shoved it whole in his mouth."

Dad laughed.

The restaurant looked closed, but a quick push on the door said otherwise. We went in and a beautiful eighteen-year-old girl came to seat us.

Dad asked in Basque, "Give me one beer."

She looked at him, puzzled. "I don't speak Euskara."

"You not from here?" Dad retorted in surprise.

"No, from Madrid." Had we been more attentive, we would have noticed the darker skin and almond eyes that gave her away as someone from farther south.

"Why you come up here?"

"For work," she said.

All through our meal, Dad seemed slightly irritated by this revelation.

"Do you know where to find Gernikako Arbola?" I asked while paying the bill. She furrowed her thin brow.

"The tree—the Tree of Gernika. Do you know where it is?"

"She don' know." Dad showed contempt.

We went to a bar around the corner for directions and found a woman and a young man behind the counter, the latter not of drinking age but serving up wine and beer as a skilled veteran.

"Arbol Foral, dónde está?" I asked. From them came the same clueless hesitation.

"The Tree of Gernika—do you know where it is?"

"We're not from here," they said while drying shot glasses.

"Oh, Jesus Christ," Dad blurted, his contempt turning finally to anger.

An old man from the end of the bar overheard our question and motioned for us to follow him outside.

By a bench next to a dozing woman, the man pointed to steps across the street rising above the nonfunctioning ground clock. He couldn't speak, though his lips exaggerated movement like a first grader sounding out words from a storybook. From his gaping mouth came quick, jerky chirps like a hamster in a cage—*hic, tic, bic, kic*—seemingly random pronouncements, ghosts of words, as spittle dripped down his chin and he wiped it with a kerchief.

"What de hell wrong with you?"

"Dad!" I scolded, hitting him in the arm.

I thanked the old man and we made our way in the direction of his pointing finger.

"What wrong with him?"

"I think he lost his larynx, his voice box. Maybe he smoked too much and they had to take it out."

"Well, Jesus Christ. Only one ol' man who know anyding and he don' say one fuckin' word." And then mockingly, Dad pointed and imitated the *hics* and *tics* and *bics* and *kics* of the kind old man who showed us the way.

"Dad, be nice," and I hit him in the arm again.

Gernikako Arbola, Gernika's famous tree, came into view atop the stairs. It was not a colossal specimen on par with a sequoia, but rather a mere sapling surrounded by a quaint wrought-iron fence between the Casa de Juntas on one side and Iglesia de Santa Maria on the other. The sapling had been grown from a shoot off the larger oak, now a big stump encased honorably behind a gazebo of white columns. Dad took a picture by it. The stump held the history and dreams of the people who endured Gernika's bombing and later found meaning in a tree, a church, and an assembly hall that did not fall under the brimstone of Franco's Armageddon.

The sapling was a new generation, still growing and waiting to make its mark, live its history, and symbolize dreams of younger people, some living, some yet unborn. How it grew—to what height or girth or depth of root— remained a mystery, for it drew nourishment from Basque life all around, there in Gernika and now from diasporas scattered like leaves around the globe. Without deep roots and proper tending, the mightiest of all things simply toppled.

Looking down from the oak, I tried to imagine the night when the bombs razed the buildings and homes and drowned people and animals in smoke and fire. Anything I conjured seemed pitifully weak compared to the reality. A museum nearby retold the story, but I feared that many, if not most, had forgotten, including those living in Spain, or those living abroad who by blood linked to this town, or all others who by common humanity tolerated bomb- ings akin to Gernika's night of terror.

Yes, the sapling had to grow and would grow, but in that pure air on Gerni- ka's sacred hill, I wondered if meaning would grow too and not fall.

"You need a nap?" I asked Dad.

" 'Bout dat time."

Dad slept for two hours while I explored Gernika's marketplace, a spiral canopy where goods were sold every Monday, as in olden days. Today, a Tuesday, the market sat quiet and empty except for stray boxes, crates, and a few blood spatters at one end. Old people lining the market's rim outside dozed in place. Had Dad lived here, he would have been among them.

Back at the hotel, he had woken. "I bought tickets for tonight," I told him.

"Tickets for what?"

"A pelota match."

"Here? Tonight?"

"That's right."

"Dere's goin' to be one crowd."

"We'll get there early."

"How far away?"

"Just a couple blocks. We can walk." He squinched his nose. I knew his hip ached.

"How about we drive over," I said, "and then we can find a restaurant after."

"You not find one parking spot."

"Let me worry about that."

At the small event center, I dropped Dad at the front entrance and watched him limp the short distance to the door, and then I found parking across the street.

"You sure dere's one tournament here?" It seemed terminally quiet.

"I'm sure. I bought tickets here," I said, thumbing at the window behind us.

"I don' think so."

In the audience, I counted twelve people—all old men—dressed in white shirts and dark jackets, each one holding a cane or needing a cane, some with hearing aids or wearing glasses, and all lugging well-fed bellies like Dad's. Unlike the men on the park benches, these men gestured in the air and raised their canes to ferry the players up and down the court, willing them to make a point or fall on their faces.

The two teams of two players each had short, broad shoulders and a hint of belly. They caught the pelota in their wicker baskets and hurled it to the wall, as the other team positioned for a return.

The old men bet on each point and yelled obscenities at one another like old friends after so many years of kidding and teasing and feeling comfortable that nothing said would be taken with malice.

In the end, the red team won the evening with impressive acrobatic skill.

"Dat was damn good," Dad said.

"Glad you liked it."

I pulled the car around, as Dad's limp made him wince with pain. Up and down we drove Gernika's main road in search of a restaurant, but the few we found had been closed for hours.

"We might have to go to bed hungry, Dad."

"Over dere!" He hit me in the arm and pointed to a small neon-lit café a block over. "Go dere."

The menu showed a selection of noodles and tempura, white or brown rice, and two or three types of sushi. Dad's eyes wandered around the room. A lone Japanese man sucked long noodles from a bowl using chopsticks to heap them into his mouth. A look of contempt twisted Dad's face.

"Dis not Basco."

"No, it's not—Japanese."

"You order for me."

He found a seat and I came to the table with bowls of rice, shrimp, broccoli, and thinly sliced and boiled chicken.

"No. No. Dis not right."

"This is the best they had, Dad. I got you a fork too."

He skewered another pointed glance at the Japanese man and his noodles, scooped two bites of rice, chewed a shrimp down to the tail, and then pushed the bowl away.

"Aren't you hungry?"

"No," and he folded his arms.

"Are you feeling okay?"

"I feel fine," and then he turned sideways in his chair, admiring nothing, much like the stare of the old people on the benches.

Lying in bed that night, he said, "I never think I see de day."

"What day is that?" I already knew what lurked in his thoughts.

"When dey got one Japanese place here."

"What's wrong with Japanese places?"

"Noding wrong. Fine. Good." He elongated the words for effect. "But—see if you understand me—dis place—I don' know how to say—dis place, Basco everyding. Euskadi everyding. If no Basco here, you no find dem no place. If Basco you lose here, you lose dem every place."

I sensed his concern and empathized.

"It'll be okay, Dad," I said, though I couldn't be sure of that. "Just get some sleep."

I lay awake feeling Dad's sense about Gernika. Though beautiful and charming, warm and inviting, proud and historic, it gave no sense of a city on the rise or of a people in the throes of a population explosion—twelve old men wielding canes, old women dozing on benches, young people not knowing of the oak or Euskara, or new ethnicities creeping in. It felt tired and worn, as though twilight had settled in, a gray convalescence where everyone lived comfortably but at the end of their days. If Gernika truly represented *Basco everyding,* then the hourglass had more sand below than above, as it did for Dad and his generation.

I lay awake thinking sadly of this. But I reasoned too that as old Basco faded away, and my dad's generation with it, a new kind of Basco had begun to rise from the ashes, one that adhered, I hoped, to the best parts of the old while defining something new, a feat that seemed both daunting and embryonic.

From the other bed came snores and then a dreamy, unsettling mumble. I waited for the dawn.

# 6

"You go and learn." That's what Dad's mother told him after Spain's Civil War ended.

When he told my mom, "He got to learn," many decades later, I believed the sentiment was original, not realizing that it had come from Grandma.

A quiet old nun had secretly opened a schoolhouse in Lekeitio. The regular school had been closed soon after Franco's victory and turned into barracks for troops. The new school was a single room, packed with ten or twelve long tables with chairs on all sides and children of varying ages sitting in them. Dirt had broken through rotting planks on the floor and two windows had been boarded up, leaving only one for light. The ceiling leaked. A chalkboard swiveled on wheels. No chalk.

At the front of the room, the nun in habit—a generational predecessor to Sister Mary Kathleen and Sister Dennis—wore a black patch over one eye. She had lost the eye to disease or to the regime—no one knew which. Her skin hung two sizes too big on her frame, all wrinkled like elephant hide, bunching up and sagging under the arms and at the jowls. Short in stature, strict, disciplined, with a voice that had one volume—loud—she barked commands like a general in a field of battle.

A hundred children, mostly young boys, crammed into that single room. If a boy misbehaved, she pressed her face an inch from his nose and stared him down with her one good eye, which dripped pus from an infected cataract. She scowled at him with a frog frown and furrowed her brows into a caterpillar. Coarse whiskers stood at attention on her chin, and her breath smelled of antiseptic. Usually the boy shaped up right away. If not, she reached her bony hand up to the patch and flashed the vacant socket underneath. After that discipline, some boys didn't return. Those who did never fell out of line again. Scared of the empty-socket treatment, Dad opted to be mindful and studious.

The one-eyed nun educated them once a week. Each student received a piece of paper, and every two of them shared a pencil. If it needed sharpening, she pulled a small penknife from under her black robe and shaved the end until the lead poked through. Most of the pencils had been scraped to the nub. The paper was secondhand and cut or torn into different sizes. If it hadn't been used in the classroom, it would have been used at the toilet.

"She keep one or two teaching books," Dad recalled. "We all use de same one, and den when I got done, de next one, he use it, and so we all learn de book. Den she say a word and she say, 'Okay, now, you spell dat,' and so I spell dat word, and den she do anoder word and anoder. Pretty soon, I learnt dem words."

Dad borrowed a book when he could, traced his finger over the letters, and memorized the curves and angles. He took extra care not to bend the yellowed pages.

He did not know the old nun's name. Anonymity offered safety. She wore her black and white habit, pulled snugly around her one-eyed face, as a double-edged fashion. It gave her protection born of piety, poverty, and the church. But it also marked her in a crowd and drew unwanted eyes, a condition she desperately tried to avoid since she carried contraband blood in her veins. To educate a Basque child was not officially a crime, but teaching or speaking the Basque language or extolling the virtues of Basque culture and heritage carried stiff punishment as the state saw fit. Franco cast a wide gray shadow.

Dad showed up at the schoolroom one day at the appointed time, on time as always, and the nun was not there. He looked for her, inquired about her. Where was she? No one knew. Had anyone seen her? No one had. Did she say where she was going? She hadn't. He moped home. He checked the school-house every day for several weeks, and each time, it was empty.

"She a good woman," Dad said in remembrance.

He paused and looked at his own blue-veined hands spotted with age. Intensity came over him. He reached deep into the grayness to find a look—the wideness of her good eye, the color of her patch, the wrinkle of her cheeks, the curve of her nose, the contour of her lips. He wanted to grab and hold the sister's face as though studying a photograph. He traveled in his own mind, passing image after image, aware yet not part of the scene.

He then said pensively, "I don' 'member her no more."

Dad lived in Gizaburuaga, about seven miles from Lekeitio, on a farm with his parents, one brother, and three sisters. Later, another brother and sister would be added to this brood. Without his classes, he stayed on the family farm, tending sheep and goats, collecting wood, and carving lumber from the pines. He dared not risk boredom, which dulled alertness and vigilance. Franco had stationed soldiers in most Basque towns. They monitored anyone or anything suspicious; that became their job.

"You fin' one on every street corner," Dad said. They dressed in dark fatigues, caps pulled low to shroud the eyes, and ankle boots with pant cuffs tucked in. With guns slung over their shoulders and few rules of engagement, they shot people in the early days for small offenses and gained reputations as roaming ghost-makers.

A man drafted by Franco was a reluctant participant at first. He still carried the social graces and kindnesses of a Spanish citizen. He offered "please" and "thank you" as a matter of course and retained manners to the extent that he had them. He told stories of home and family, fishing or farming, and dreamt of tilling and hoeing a piece of soil or owning his own boat to bring in a catch. He walked carefree as he had before the draft and moved aside in the street if a lady happened his way. But no one heard his stories or pleasantries. No one acknowledged his kindnesses or his manners. The people focused on the uniform, the scruffy boots, the gun. The soldier had power and he soon realized it.

A mouse trained a thousand times to push a button abandoned the charge once offered a piece of cheese. His nature demanded it. A soldier was the same. He learned kindness and manners to use in civil company. But dangle a little power before him and he became a mouse after the cheese. His nature demanded it. To resist defied evolution. The exception proved the rule.

Before the war, residents of Lekeitio brought goods to market. Fishermen netted cod or halibut, filleted it and rolled it in salt, and set it out. Half a peseta bought one piece, a whole peseta bought three. The farmers harvested corn and carrots and potatoes, cut lumber, and bundled sticks for burning in iron stoves. They wrung the necks of geese, butchered lambs for chops and mutton, plucked chickens or sold eggs, and skinned rabbits and hung them on hooks.

Dad helped his father sell bread and milk. He displayed long, thin loaves with tough crusts and wrapped a full inventory in towels to keep it warm and fresh. A loaf sold for a tenth of one peseta, not more than a dime. On Saturday mornings, he picked up empty bottles in front of select doors in town, and then on Sunday, he milked two goats, bottled it, and delivered it. Milk on the Sabbath seemed to be a Catholic exception, maybe in deference to the Virgin Mary. Dad made a run once a week, careful not to spill or break the glass. To do so voided a week's wages and then someone in the family, maybe himself, went hungry until the goats produced again.

In the marketplace, patrons mingled among the commerce, took a loaf, a bottle of milk, a tomato or carrot, a lump of mutton, or a piece of cod. Residents bargained for profit while carrying home food and supplies to last a week.

The model changed after the war. Franco declared the Basque provinces of Bizkaia and Gipuzkoa to be traitor provinces and exacted heavier taxes from them. Farmers had to turn in milk from the goats, bread from the ovens, vegetables from the gardens, and lamb from the fields. Soldiers took the items to town and set prices differently each week, usually too high. Families received a stipend to live, though many did not get theirs and those who did complained of its meager size.

"Dey come 'round," Dad said, "and take eggs or chicken. Don' matter what. They take it all. And what can you do? Daddy give it to dem."

Items were sold from a central location in Lekeitio or placed in wagons and trucks and shipped elsewhere in the country. Guards watched each transaction and periodically pocketed a half peseta or more for every two or three paid to the state.

A black market developed overnight. Residents hid their food stores, livestock, woven cloth, carved buttons, and anything of value under floorboards or in walls, underground or in barns. They monitored for weeks who might be friend or foe before agreeing to a transaction. "Spies all over," Dad said. Then they transacted business under cover of night, in the woods away from town or at temporary roving sites on the outskirts of Lekeitio. "You look over your shoulder—got to." Eventually, so much seeped out of the controlled economy that soldiers inspected nearly anyone who entered the town center and roamed the surrounding countryside to collect goods at their source of production.

Dad had to be unsuspicious. He did not make eye contact with the soldiers. The eyes were a window to the soul; better to keep one's soul under wraps and cast eyes downward. He never ran. Sudden moves invited attention. He did not wear fine clothes, show money, or boast. In these instances, his worries remained small. His Sunday best looked very much like all of his other outfits—holey trousers, faded undersized shirts, laceless mismatched shoes or bare feet, all hand-me-downs through his brother Juan, a neighbor, or his father. His penniless pockets were the least-worn parts of his trousers, giving him nothing to boast about. Mostly, as a boy and not a girl, he did not attract the unwanted eyes of young soldiers.

Among his family, his mom and dad—frisked. They did not attempt to conceal or sell anything outside the controlling eyes of the guards. His sister Isabella, much older than he was, and closer to adulthood than childhood, with thick dark hair, brown eyes, eggshell skin, and a well-groomed, shapely figure, drew the hormonal instincts of the young guards. She followed her parents' example. Another sister, Fakunda, younger than Isabella, had forming breasts and widening hips. Any hope of passing young soldiers unannounced became increasingly risky.

The older brother, Juan, posed a different risk. Entering his mid-teen years, he had become a threat to anyone in uniform, an object of suspicion and equally an opportunity for a soldier to show his authority and superiority by frisking this un-enlisted, un-drafted boy. Juan avoided town as much as he could.

Anita was the only one left. She resembled Dad, with a large nose, brown eyes, and wide forehead. Her shoulders, not as wide as his, still broadened uncommonly wide for a girl of her age. She did not show the sprouting signs of womanhood like Isabella and Fukunda, nor offer a masculine threat as Tío Juan did. Her path carried less risk, though it was not risk-free.

Anita rode a donkey one day out of town with sacks of grain on its back. She passed a group of soldiers standing in a doorway, each of them smoking a cigarette, talking, and paying little attention. In front of them, the donkey lurched and one of the grain bags fell from its back. She jumped down, but couldn't budge it, and the donkey, so often a four-legged stubborn beast, moved in one direction or another, adding to her frustrations. The soldiers watched until one of them went to her as the others whistled behind him.

"What you got in there?" He blew smoke from nose and mouth.

Anita dropped the bag. "Nothing." She did not make eye contact, kept her head down, and interlaced her fingers meekly.

"Must be something. Let's see, sweet one."

Holding the cigarette between his lips, the soldier swung his gun to his back and unsheathed a knife from his belt. He held it in front of her and Anita saw the gleam of the blade. Then, looking straight at her, he stabbed the knife forcefully into the bag, opened a wide slit, and rummaged inside. He pulled out a handful of grain and tossed it around, then another handful and another, until the bag was empty. The donkey dipped its head low and licked up the oats.

"You're right." He blew smoke. "Nothing here, sweet one." He touched her cheek with his thumb, resheathed the knife, and swaggered back to the doorway.

Anita frantically scooped the grain with her small hands and thrust it into the shredded bag, but most of it had scattered in the dirt. Tears streamed down and made wet spots on the burlap. Her hands trembled. She heard laughter from behind and felt certain that it was aimed at her. She cried harder and then she became terrified. Hoisting the lighter bag to the hindquarters of the donkey, she grabbed the harness at its nose and pulled the stubborn beast down the road to home. The laughter faded as she made distance, but in her dreams she heard the cackle of the guards, felt the touch of the thumb, and saw the glare of the blade. It all stayed with her for a long time.

Dad knew this. He and Anita shared nearly everything. They kept little from each other. When Anita didn't want to go into town, Dad felt that he could not force her. In the past, they had often gone together, and with a quarter peseta bought a piece of chocolate to share before going home. But Dad's only companion now was a donkey.

"What was the donkey's name?" I once asked him.

He paused and smiled and with a shoulder shrug replied, "Jackass."

All alone, he expected to be more clever than Anita and less suspicious. Going into town became part chore, part game, part challenge to evade the guards, sell bread or pick up goods, and get home.

Every day he got better at the game. He tied loaves of bread flat against the donkey. On top, he packed a tangled mass of thorny stems and sticks. Any guard who pushed a searching arm inside pulled back bloody scratches.

Dad rode the donkey to a secluded place well outside the town center. He found a plot of powdered dirt where a fifteen-foot pole, anchored in the ground, held a crucifix at the top. He unfurled his loaves next to it and quietly sold bread at a fair price. The guards did not come around.

Afterward, he shopped in town. He tossed away the prickly sticks that had shrouded his bread and then loaded up his donkey. He made sure not to pack anything he couldn't lift. Passing the guards on the way home, he turned back to stare at them. They puffed on their cigarettes, laughed, and patted each other's shoulders. So in control they seemed, standing in those doorways. He planned to tell Anita everything when he got home. Together in the dark of their room, they would share a piece of chocolate that he had bought with extra money.

———— ∞ ————

Where Dad lived in Gizaburuaga, the land grew thick with pine and oak. Each month soldiers came to confiscate the wood, and in return Grandpa got a paltry supplement to the family's stipend. He packed a few rotting logs in with the good ones as a silent protest, hoping that somewhere at some point one of those rotting logs would give Franco or his minions a little trouble. That made his heart glad.

Everyone kept busy collecting wood, tending sheep and goats, baking bread, or preparing meals. The sun rose, work done, meals served, the sun set, and bedtime came. That was the cycle of daily life. Only a secret visit to town to sell bread or milk broke the monotony.

In the dampness of autumn and the cold of winter, the family gathered in the kitchen, the warmest room of the house. They took meals there and spent hours in conversation after the last heel of bread and drizzle of wine. Grandpa talked as everyone crouched around the table. No one spoke unless spoken to. Anything mentioned between kitchen walls—Franco and the government, plans to circumvent soldiers, stashes of money—lived and died in that warm room. A bond formed among them, one of trust and respect, of honor and family, and of love. After hours of listening to Grandpa's slow voice, the children scampered to bed with subtle tales of subversion dancing in their dreams. I imagined that if heaven offered the smallest glimpse here on earth, it would be a large family in a small kitchen exchanging stories, feeling love, and eating warm bread.

On Sundays, Grandma made pudding from goat's milk and leftover rice. The brothers and sisters clutched spoons in anticipation, and as she plopped the dessert on the table, it triggered a frenzy of stabbing into the bowl. Etiquette be damned! Each fended for himself. Servings derived solely from utensil size, elbow speed, and gullet width, a type of natural selection, *Basco desserticus*.

One time as Grandma set the bowl down and wild arms and clinging utensils dug in, Anita found herself without a spoon. She scoured the drawer, the sink, the cupboard—all empty. She scurried back, pushed between Dad and Juan, ladled her hand into the bowl, and slurped rice and milk from her palm.

The delicacy dripped from her fingers and down her chin. The crashing of spoons didn't end until the bowl looked freshly washed. Then they all returned to a week of bland, dessert-less meals.

"We dream dat jus' once we each get one bowl of *arroz con leche* our own. But dere only one bowl each week, and sometimes Momma and Daddy, dey put noding on the table, so we go to bed hungry. I tell Anita, 'I think I goin' to die,' and she give me one piece of her bread de next morning."

They cared for each other. Trusting no one outside the family became an act of survival. Once when soldiers from Lekeitio came to Gizaburuaga to collect lumber, Grandpa and Juan stacked it in their truck like dutiful citizens, took the extra stipend, and closed the tailgate for the soldiers to be on their way.

One of the soldiers asked Grandpa, "How old your boy?"

"He's fourteen." He lied outright and didn't twitch or avert the eyes or blink. He had played enough *mus* to know how to bluff under pressure. Had the Catholic sisters of my youth witnessed Grandpa's blatant dishonesty, they might have pursed their lips and scowled with disappointment. But Grandpa too knew about greater goods and believed the question represented more than a casual interest in Juan's age.

The soldier came back powerfully, "You sure 'bout that? He looks older."

"He's my boy. I know." Grandpa held his ground.

The two soldiers backed away, got in their truck, and drove away as Grandpa and Juan watched the cloud of dirt trail their wheels.

Dad didn't know when Grandpa first thought of sending his boys to America, but this moment qualified as a prime candidate. Humans expected to struggle, and through persistent defeat they learned, built, and became more. But turn their futures dark and bleak, snuff out dreams, press them over a line from struggle to despair, and it triggers a basic instinct deep in the fiber among the chromosomes to climb, to rise, to escape. The only human sense more powerful is the one felt by a father for a son.

———⟋⟍———

Vicente Juaristi spent months at sea before hitting San Francisco's port in 1890. He and the crew had survived on limes and plums and had come ashore weighing nearly forty pounds lighter, though scurvy had not set in. On horse-back, Vicente climbed the Sierras into Carson City and crossed the sagebrush plains to Elko. Nearly dead from the trip, he signed on at a sheepherding camp, got three squares per day and a few pennies for his pocket. Over twenty years, he saved to bring his brother Mariano Juaristi, Dad's father, to the States.

Grandpa had been in the United States first in 1910 for nearly a year and then again in 1920. Both times he passed through Ellis Island and made his way across the continent to meet his brother in Elko. Vicente had dreamt of establishing a ranch with his brother, my grandpa, and becoming a cattle tycoon. The dream never took and he did not get rich, but he had food and a roof, a job and a place to lay his head at night.

Grandpa told Dad of this fabled place called "Amerika." He told of buildings that blocked the sun, automobiles in the streets, men in suits, and food and wine aplenty. He told of prairies thick with thousands of sheep and cattle and wild horses running free, schools open for all, and enough work for every man to have his pick of one or two jobs if he wanted them. Why wouldn't any man want to work as much as he could?

When Dad turned sixteen, his brother Juan had already been in Franco's army for more than three years. "It make Daddy sick in his belly to see Juan in dat uniform," said Dad, "but he go. He got no choice, and Daddy, he don' know if Juan, he live or he die, he jus' go away for long time."

Fortunately, Dad looked younger than Juan at the same age that he had been drafted. Soldiers who came for lumber did not ask questions, but Dad and Grandpa knew that they couldn't outwit the soldiers for another year, so Grandpa reached out to his brother, who was still in Elko. Vicente agreed to sponsor Dad's passage.

On his last night in Spain, he thought of what his father had told him. "Amedica was a place," he said, "where a man, he can work hard and do somding with himself, and if you work, you got money in your pocket, and no one never can take dat from you."

The next morning he ate bread and potatoes, more than he enjoyed usually over three or four days. Grandma made him his own bowl of rice pudding, and he ended up sharing it with Anita, who cried while slurping the milk. Grandpa took him to town to catch a bus for Bilbao, where he would fly to Madrid and, from there, to the United States to take up a new charge as a young sheep-herder. Vicente sent money to pay for the flight, a wad of cash to bribe Franco's authorities out of Spain, and an extra five dollars to fill Dad's pocket before he left home. In Bilbao, Dad boarded and looked out the window. It was his first ride on a bus, his first trip out of Lekeitio, his first dream beyond Spain. He would remember the moment, December 1947, and carry it with him for all time.

"I go to Amedica," he said, "to do what oders do, to work, to be bigger, to do someding, and den I call dat my own."

## 7

"Dis so pretty," Dad said.

We had traveled twenty miles west of Bilbao toward Laredo on Spain's northern coast. After our stay in Gernika, I looked forward to exploring new scenery, architecture, and small hamlets that grew more Spanish and less Basque the farther west we drove. The buildings slowly lost red clay roofs in favor of wood or thatch, and the distance between them shrank until, eventually, one home stacked on another into tightly pressed communities. The towns didn't lack for space, but the inhabitants seemed to prefer density over sprawl, perhaps a remnant of earlier Spanish days when conquerors came by sea, attacking citadels on the shore and forcing citizens to huddle in close quarters behind fortified walls. This mentality, born during moments of duress, did not dissipate during moments of peace, and still seemed deeply rooted among the small towns of the coastline.

The road we traveled could have been in Russia or China and Dad might not have known the difference. True, he hailed from Spain, but truer to say he hailed from a northwestern corner of Basque Country. He hadn't ventured outside his geographic nook before departing for the United States in December 1947.

He seemed now like a man thirsting for water after a desert walk, taking in everything as new and wondrous. Rolling down the windows, we inhaled the sweet perfumes of milkweed and long grass, tasted salt on our tongues, and felt sea air on our faces.

Winter firs lined the edges of plunging cliffs with white waves crashing hundreds of feet below. Geology had gotten its start along this coast. God had pressed His fingertips into the earth and pried it apart, leaving Spain in one palm and Central America in the other, the land cleaved by a great ocean in between. The cliff walls cataloged the passage of time in layers of colored sediment from prehistoric waters that flooded and receded, leaving remnants of life and traces of our origin.

"Have you ever been out here?" I asked, knowing the answer.

"No. Dis de first time." He craned his neck out his window.

"Why didn't you ever come out here?"

"What for?"

"To see all this, to see something new."

"I seeing it now."

I sensed no regret for not exploring these lush hillsides over a single mountain opposite his childhood home.

"Imagine all the people you would've met," I suggested.

"Like what kinda people?"

"What do you mean, 'What kind of people?' Any kind. All kinds."

"What for? No Bascos come here."

"To meet and talk to different people, to learn about them, what they like and don't like, and how they live."

"Bah!" He grunted. "Maybe I come out here, and den I never leave Spain and den you never been born. Bascos, dey stay to demselves."

When I was growing up, Dad represented my first and largely only exposure to all things Basque. He became my baseline, a rule against which I compared all other Basque encounters. Mentally, I marked any variations to this baseline as an exception to the Basque archetype, but over time the variations mounted until finally Dad became the exception—a tough admission for a son to make of his father. Soon the variations formed or at least had begun to form a new Basque identity, a new baseline.

I marveled at how Dad's truth no longer represented the truth around him. As a seafaring people, the Basques had ventured farther and farther from Spanish shores in search of fish or the perfect whale. Evidence placed them on Canadian shores as early as the sixteenth century. As Spain colonized the New World, the Basques joined crews as expert navigators and seamen, making them some of the earliest Europeans to touch South American soil. They found honored places among the crews of Columbus and Magellan.

As an upset to history, in fact, Magellan did not circumnavigate the globe. He died about halfway, in the Philippines during the Battle of Mactan. A Basque navigator, Juan Sebastian Elkano, took the wheel after Magellan died and led his men the rest of the way home, an achievement often overlooked in the annals of early navigational history.

The Basques sprinkled themselves throughout the New World before Spain's Civil War, but Dad's belief that "Bascos, dey stay to demselves," still held reasonable validity into the early twentieth century. They seemed to cultivate a fierce independence that clung to autonomy, self-determination, and a desire to live freely or, more aptly, to be left alone. After the Spanish Civil War, political exile pushed them out and opportunities abroad pulled them in. More than 150,000 Basques, like Dad, left their homeland and emigrated to escape conscription, the harsh treatment of Franco's programs, or the miserable poverty and feelings of economic desperation.

Now, sixty years later, the Basques have spread to more than twenty countries, as far away as Australia and with strong concentrations in Argentina, the United States, Venezuela, and Uruguay. These and other countries have launched more than 150 official Basque centers to study and focus Basque culture and custom. Dad didn't know about this new truth, and he wouldn't have cared about it if he had learned it. His truth remained frozen, kindly, gently, in a comfortable past.

"Haven't you missed a lot by sticking to yourself?" I asked him.

"What you mean?"

"I mean don't you think you could have had more opportunities if you were more curious, ventured out here, and explored?"

"If you too curious, you get in trouble."

"How so?"

"See if you understand. If you go looking for someding, you find it. And den pretty soon, what you find, it change you."

"Isn't that a good thing?"

"Depends what you give up."

"Why do you have to give up anything?"

"Because you find someding and it change you, and den someding else, it get lost."

"That's probably true."

"Damn right, it's truth! Basque—Euskara—it been 'round long, long time, oldest language in Europe. It been de same for a thousand years, maybe longer. It survive 'cause it pass from grandpa to daddy to boy. Dey don' write it down. Dat keep it de same."

"I think that it's been written down now, Dad."

"No, dey didn't."

"I think they did."

"If dey did, dat's one mistake." He raised a finger to accentuate the point. "You 'member dat story that Grandma tell and I tell you?"

"Which one?"

"De one 'bout de devil."

"Yes."

"What dat story say?"

"The devil traveled the world looking for souls to corrupt. He sought to pull the very best innocent souls to evil, which would give him strength by lessening goodness in the world. When he found these innocents, he learned their language and then whispered in their ears all day and night. He whispered of greed and envy, and gluttony and lust, and sloth and wrath, and worst of all, pride. He had time on his side, so he didn't care how long it took; he wore down any innocent who thought himself strong enough to resist. He provoked people into their sins, tempted them, every day, every hour, every minute until they gave in. After he turned them from lightness to darkness, he felt his heart swell and then left to find another people to corrupt."

"Yes, dat's right," Dad said. "And what happen when he come to de Basque?"

"When the devil came to the Basques, as he had with so many others, he began to learn their language. He stayed among the people for a week, a month, a year, a hundred years. Yet after all that time, the devil could not grasp the Basque tongue, learning only *bai* for 'yes' and *ez* for 'no.' With that limited knowledge, he tried to move the Basques to sin, but he failed for the first time since his banishment from heaven. In disgust, he left Euskadi, never to return, which explains why to this day the Basques are a good and virtuous people largely without sin."

"You tell dat good. I like dat story."

"Seems a little prideful, if you ask me."

"You mark my words," he said, ignoring me. "If dey write down Euskara, dey tear it apart. Pretty soon, little by little, it sound like Spanish or French or someding else. Everyding going to sound just the same."

"Maybe then we can all talk to each other," I suggested mischievously.

"I don' want to talk to nobody except who I want to talk to."

I smiled at him and popped Mozart into the CD player as we moved along the coast.

"What dis noise?"

"It's Mozart, Dad."

"Bah!" He wrinkled his nose and turned to the window.

In Laredo, traffic stalled. It appeared to be a permanent condition, not a surge of rush hour traffic. The foundations of old Europe clogged the movement—cobblestones, rock structures, central water wells, fortified castle walls. Crowds overflowed into narrow streets from even narrower sidewalks. Overhead neon and product signs gave an impression of clutter.

"So dirty here." Dad crinkled his nose with disdain. "People, dey all stacked up like one pile of sardines."

We inched down single-lane alleys, through a crush of bodies. Hands brushed the side windows and feet kicked the rear bumper. We felt like pieces of chocolate tossed on an anthill.

"You see all dem damn people? Pretty soon, dere's going to be too many people. Den what the hell we do?"

"What do you mean?"

"All dose people, dey need one place to live, food, water, little wine. Not enough go 'round."

"I think you're right."

"How many people dere are now?"

"In the whole world?"

"Yes."

"About six and a half billion."

"You say billion?"

"Yes."

"Jesus Christ, dere's dat many? World no able to support dat."

"And the number keeps going up," I told him. "In my life, there will be ten billion or more on the planet."

"No dere won't."

"Yes, there will, Dad."

"Dey kill each oder first. Dey blow each oder up and den, good-bye, Charlie."

"You don't think we can get along?"

"Hell no."

"We get along in the United States."

"People dey got to give up lots of dings, and dey won't. And if dey don't give up, den dey kill each oder."

"Give up what?"

"Everyding—big house, one ranch, acreage, eat, eat, eat all day long. Dey got to live in one room with one bowl of food. Dat's it. People no give up all dose dings."

"You talk like everyone's Basque, Dad."

"De Basque never give up dose dings. Lots oders won't either. Who want to live like dat?"

"Maybe we don't have to give up much. Maybe each of us gives up a little bit."

"Some people, dey don' got noding to give. Dey don' got one pot to piss in. Den oder people, dey got too much. Dey're de ones who won't let go. Dey got everyding already."

"You make it sound hopeless."

"What you mean?"

"You sound like there's no hope, that we'll get more and more people until we finally kill each other off."

"If we got war now—what you say?—with six billion people, you think we get less war with ten or twenty billion? You crazy."

"You're probably right. But we don't need to think about it. I don't even know how we got on the subject."

"Dat God damn place. What de hell de name?"

"Laredo."

"Yes, Fuckin' Laredo. Dat's why de Basque, dey stay home." With that, he stubbornly turned away, a little heated, to look out his window. He began to whistle and I knew I had lost him for the afternoon.

I recognized his melody. It didn't have a name, at least none that I knew, but it was one of a hundred that he whistled when he became contemplative. I had heard all of them. They rivaled Euskara in age but, to my knowledge, had not been translated into sheet music.

Surprisingly, I heard in his tune a variation on a theme, Mozart's *Eine Kleine Nachtmusik,* taken from the CD playing softly in our Subaru. Threads had been woven cleverly into Dad's ancient Basque melody.

"What are you whistling?" I asked.

Without looking at me, he said, "One Basque song."

I turned off the CD to listen and wondered if the new rendition gained in stature or if something special had been lost.

# 8

In 1910, Dad's father, Mariano, boarded a ship bound for America where his only brother, Vicente, had established himself as a reliable ranch hand, the masterful sheepherder, horseshoer, calf roper, fence builder, barn fixer, and trusted friend. Mariano planned to join him on his ranch, earn money, and send it home to feed a growing number of mouths. Mariano had two babies at this point, with another five, including Dad in 1930, to come about over the next twenty-five years.

Crossing the Atlantic, one of the passengers coughed and within a day or two the passengers writhed on the deck with fever. Pale, shivering, and dizzy, Mariano retched his guts over the side, lost weight, and drowned in clothes now hanging on an emaciated body. Peering overboard into the dark deep as he heaved again and again, he might have imagined that the sea offered a welcome invitation as a final resting place.

For twenty days over rolling waves under menacing skies, Mariano questioned his decision to leave Spain. When he thought his circumstance could not worsen, the clouds opened, rain fell, and a cold humidity touched his bones, adding to the gloom and despair of his illness.

Then in the distance, beyond mist rising from calmer waters, in the chill of early dawn, he spied a lady crowned and wrapped in green, holding aloft her torch of liberty. Standing on feeble legs, he removed his old hat ringed with sweat and looked up to the New Colossus in the harbor. She invited the old to start anew. She represented hope and light and dreams fulfilled. Mariano passed through golden doors and entered upon a new land. He would stay a year and then return to Spain with a fuller view of the world and fuller pockets to care again for a wife, children, and more on the way.

His experience mirrored the romantic understanding that most Americans have of European immigrants, those huddled masses of whom Emma Lazarus so eloquently wrote, gracing our shores and yearning to breathe free. But Dad's experience forty years later held little similarity to his father's.

"Daddy, he put me on one bus from Lekeitio to Bilbao," Dad recalled of his departure in December 1947. He traveled to Madrid, a city he knew only as myth, never imagining he'd see it.

"Dere were big buildings. I didn't know you could make buildings dat big. And people like sardines packed together." He pressed his fingers to show the crush of humanity.

"I give dese guys my papers and dey stamp dem, and den I go on one military plane. . . . Brrrrrrr." He imitated the rumble of engines powering four massive propellers. "About forty guys, shoulder to shoulder, no room, and cold as a sonofabitch."

Three years after World War II, the world still salved deep wounds as a new order unfolded. An iron curtain, as Churchill predicted, was splitting the Continent. In response, America reached across the Atlantic in friendship and common cause with the Marshall Plan to restore the great powers of Europe and counter the spread of Soviet dominion.

As long as Franco ruled, Spain remained ineligible to partake of America's generosity, though several Basques like Dad, who opposed Franco, became important exceptions. These young men offered critical skills in sheepherding that America needed to keep pace with postwar demands for fine wool and other niceties.

"I sleep sitting up on dat plane, and I get dose needles in my toes and I got all crippled up," Dad continued.

"You were only seventeen, Dad. How could you get crippled up?"

"You try dat. Sit dere hours and hours, and twenty days go by, one plane, anoder plane, one bus, anoder bus. See how you feel. And it smell like shit and sweat. Aaaaawww!"

Dad growled as an expression of disgust—not moral outrage but physical queasiness. For all of his experiences gutting fish and cutting the throats of lambs, concentrated human odors, a rarity in the well-ventilated outdoors, turned his stomach.

"We go to Portugal and den all de way to Canada and Chicago and Florida and New York. I think we go to Texas too. I don' 'member all de places, too many of dem."

His circuitous route made sense. By law, the United States had frowned on military or civilian transport to or from Franco's fascist Spain, but Canada had had no such prohibitions, which might have explained why his flight landed first in Ontario and a separate flight brought him to the United States without legal objections. A similar route might be feasible today from the United States through Canada to Cuba.

"I had one loaf of bread," he said.

"Only one loaf?"

"Dat's right."

"Did you have any water or wine?"

"Hell no. I almost die on dose planes and buses. Miserable. I got to Salt Lake in twenty days, and den take one plane from dere to Elko. I got five dollars in de pocket, and one suitcase dat Momma, she pack for me. When I seen Elko, I couldn't believe it. In Spain, everyting green and pretty, so thick with trees, mountains all round, ocean all round. Elko not de same."

Covered in sagebrush, with few trees and little water, Elko started in the late 1800s as a collection of tents along the tracks of the Western Pacific and Central Pacific Railroads, the two running side by side through the county. Unforgiving and tumbling with weeds, the terrain crawled with rattlesnakes. Soft hands turned hard, became calloused and gnarled, with blackened thumbs and broken knuckles. Winters lasted sometimes nine months, with snowfall reaching at times over five feet. Stories of the Donner Party still held sway, and men seeking their fortune passed cautiously through the Sierras en route to the golden promise of California.

A fair balance of ranching and mining interests had congregated around Elko, with ranching hitting a peak following World War II as Dad arrived in town. A few years before, a new post office had been built to continue Elko's early history with the Pony Express. Later that same year, Dad would see five doctors—Hood, Hadfield, Secor, Collett, and Moren—come together to christen Elko's first clinic.

The two railroads still ran through town between Elko's main establishments—the Stockmen's and the Commercial—where temporary labor and ranch hands found a room and ate a steak, and then hopped a boxcar and disappeared to their next work stop. But Dad spent little time in town.

"My uncle Vicente, he put me to work," he said. "We go to his ranch and dat same night I work. Sonofabitch. I so tired. Just get dere and I go right to work."

"What did you do?"

"I do everyding—feed de lambs, fix one fence, cut de firewood, feed de chickens. I can't 'member all de things I done. If it need doing, den I did it. I even wash de dishes and clean de house. All de work. My uncle, he teach me how to herd and use de dog and keep de sheep safe. A day not go by dat I didn' lose one lamb, but 'ventually it turn up in anoder herd, and den on one oder day, I leave with one hundred sheep and I come back with one hundred and ten, so I pick up ten from someplace. It all come out."

After a few months apprenticed to his uncle, Dad spent nights alone with the herd. Beneath a sky of stars, lying by a campfire, eating beans and drinking coffee, he conjured up images of home—a family farmhouse atop a hill in Gizaburuaga, Gernika's sacred oak, boats bobbing at dock, fish guts and brine. He saw faces of family, green valleys and tall mountains shrouded in clouds.

"Some of the sheepherders," he said, "dey cry and cry for deir momma or daddy, and some of dem, dey just quit and go back to Spain."

"But you didn't. Why not?"

"After a year, my uncle, he send me to de Smith Brothers to work, and I make more money. And den I go work for Sorenson's and Jess Goicoechea. Each time I go one place to anoder, I make a little more, so I stay here in dis country. Noding back in Spain—no jobs, no food, no noding for me dere. You know what?"

"What?"

"I almos' go to Korea. You know dat?"

"No, I didn't know that. You mean from the United States?"

"Dat's right."

"How'd that happen?"

"One day at Sorenson's ranch, prob'ly 1950 or '51, dese men, dey come from the government and dey tell us dat we got to go to Korea to fight one war. We don' know about no war. But dey round up all de sheepherders and put us on one train and take us to Salt Lake. I stay dere three days in one room, about fifteen of us sleep on de ground. Den Sorenson, he go to Carson City or Washington, DC, I don't know, and he raise hell about what dese government men done. He give one helluva speech, I guess, and tell dem big shots to let go of his workers. And after three days, dey put us on de train and send us back to Elko. Den it was over."

"I imagine that scared you," I said.

"You betcha," he replied. "One bullet, and good-bye, Charlie. I think den— see if you understand me—for de first time—first time—dis place, here in dis country, not Spain, dis place my home. You go to war—dat scare me—but you got to go if dat's your home."

"I understand, Dad."

"Den after dat, I decide to get my citizenship papers. I learn English best I can, and I learn Spanish. I no write too good. You know, I didn' learn Spanish in Spain. Momma and Daddy, dey only talk Basco, so I come here and know only Basco. I learn Spanish in dis country. Real funny."

"That is funny." I chuckled at the irony. I knew that Dad hadn't mastered reading or writing in Basque, English, or Spanish, a fact that he hid well, especially from his children. Even the tenacity of an old nun, short and grizzled with one eye, could not push against Franco's dark tide. All children of Spain— Basque and Spanish—suffered under his regime.

"Did you stay a sheepherder for all that time, seven years?" I asked.

"No. You know, when you alone with de sheep on one mountain, you talk to one tree or one brush. You talk to de dog and you talk to de sheep. One day go by, den anoder and anoder, and you talkin', talkin', talkin' to anyding dat listens. Hard to learn English when noding talk back. Den one day, I talkin' and I think the sheep talk back to me, so I decide it time to go to town. One man go crazy out dere alone."

"So you moved into town?"

"Dat's right."

"What did you do?"

"I go work at the Star Hotel for Margarite Ozamis and husband. She pregnant and going to have one baby any time, so she need help. I work dere bussing tables, tending bar, mopping de floor, doing anyding that need to be done."

"You got your citizenship while working at the Star?"

"I take de test one time and didn' pass. I couldn' read de questions good, and couldn't read de answers neither. I take the test again and I didn' pass. I get worried. I pass over seven years in dis country, so I not supposed to be here. But I try real hard. Den I take the test third time and I didn' pass third time neither."

"What did you do?"

"I paid one teacher to help me. Her name Mrs. Priester, and she say, 'Joe, if you don' pass dis time, den I'm goin' to throw de book in dat judge's face and kick his ass out of town.' I pay her thirty dollars a month and she teach me de words, de questions, de answers. She teach at one high school and she help de judge give the test, so I figure she make one good teacher. I study with her for three months every day."

"And you passed?"

"I did. I go to the test and I take it and I can't believe it, I pass dat damn thing. Den a month go by, and I stand up in front of one judge and I so nervous. He ask me, 'What your name?' and I tell him Jose Domingo Juaristi Bengoechea. Dat's how dey do it in Spain. Children take momma and daddy's names—both of dem. The judge, he say to me, 'Dat name don' fit on dis piece of paper, so I'm goin' to cut off "Bengoechea." Dat okay?' What can you say? I tell him dat okay, and dat's how my name get shrinked up. Den he tell me to raise my hand and I repeat de words he say and I sweared to dis country."

"When was that?"

"I got sweared November 1956."

"My teacher, she want me to keepa goin' with her to learn English and how to write," he continued. "But I don' have de money and so I stop. Every day, I think about dat. I should've keepa goin' with her, but I didn' know no better. She one great woman, dat one. I don' know what happen to her. She had two daughters and maybe dey still alive."

"What did you do when you became a citizen?"

"I go back to work. I work at Shorty's Club den, tending bar. I save money and get one business partner—Luigi Esnoz—and we buy de Star Hotel, just de two of us. Dat was 1959. I work terrific, terrific—day and night to keep dat business goin.' Dat's what you suppose to do. Everyding possible. Den come along de next year and I vote first time in my life."

"What did you think about that?"

"Very 'portant. I never vote for noding. I never had chance in Spain."

"Who did you vote for?"

"I vote for dat young boy, Kennedy."

"Why?"

"Why not? He talk good, look good, he young and I was young. Dat oder kokolo—what his name?" I smiled, recalling how as a boy, the word *kokolo*, meaning *idiot*, often made me laugh.

"Nixon, you mean?"

"Yes—dat kokolo. I never like him. Smart, though. He very smart man. My stomach, he tell me dat man no good. So I vote for Kennedy. Den he got shot— pobre. Sad time in dis country and 'round the world. His broder, he get shot too. De country fallin' apart, but you know what?"

"What's that, Dad?"

"Very sad when dose brothers die. But dis country stay together. Oder countries, dey go to shit. But dis country keepa goin.'"

"Pretty strong," I said.

"You God damn right," he replied.

This conversation returned to me years later when I volunteered with the Carter Center as an election observer in Nepal. The country had endured eleven years of civil war, thousands had died on both sides, but now the parties had agreed to a cease-fire long enough to hold an election for a national congress. On election day, I saw an old woman, bent like a question mark, holding a cane. She stood in line with thousands of others waiting for the polls to open. She had a deeply wrinkled face, like cracked mud, but exuded a soft kindness, a willing patience. She reminded me of Dad. Through my interpreter, I asked her age, and she said seventy-four years, maybe more. She had walked, she said, more than two hours across Himalayan hills to vote. It would be her first time. Remembering my conversation with Dad, I told her she wouldn't forget it and pulled her from the line and brought her to the front, where she hobbled into the booth and cast the first vote of the day for a new Nepal. The crowd clapped as the old woman raised her ballot in one hand and her cane in the other, both in triumph, straightened her back the best she could, and broke into a warm, toothless smile across that mud-cracked face. I thought that Dad would have been glad for her and a little proud too.

"How long did you own the Star Hotel?" I asked.

"Few years, den I sell it, and go back to Spain to see Momma and Daddy. I stay dere twenty-two months. De government dere, dey can't touch me because I'm citizen of dis country. Back den, one dollar real strong and so I live like one king in Lekeitio. But everyding different."

"How so?"

"Everyding jus' different."

"You mean Spain was different?"

"No, Spain jus' about the same. No food, no noding and Franco he still around. But I feel different dere. See if you understand me. When I come to dis country, I was seventeen and didn' know shit and den I work and I save money and become one citizen. Dat make me different. So I don' see Spain de same way. Can't. Not possible. You can't come to dis country—dis country 'specially—and den go back where you come from and not feel different."

"I understand, Dad. But then you came back to Elko."

"Dat's right. I waste so much money in Spain, and didn' do shit, just show off, dat's all, and come back here and I marry your momma and we buy the Blue Jay. Your older sister she born den and you come along couple years later. We live in de bar. You remember dat?"

"Of course I do. Do you ever miss the Old Country?"

"I don.' I miss Momma and Daddy. 'Course, dey dead now. I miss sisters— Anita 'specially—and my brother, Joakin. De mountains, trees, grass—all green and wet. I miss de little house where I growed up. I dream 'bout dat every night. I 'member it every day, and goin' in de field with Daddy. But dis country my home now. I don' want to go no place else."

"What do you like most about it?"

"Here I got you, Momma, sisters."

"Your family's here, you mean?"

"Yes, but—see if you understand me—here in dis place, you got open space

to build one house or make one ranch. You work here, dere, all over de place." His fingers punctuated the air. "You work hard, you get money. If you want to do someding you do it. If you live alone, like one sheepherder, den in dis country, you live alone and no one bother you. Dat's de difference from every place else."

## 9

An hour of whistling filled the car. Melodic, sweet, in tune, the songs poured slowly through Dad's puckered lips.

As long as I had heard them, the songs seemed heavier than air, weighed down by decades or centuries of history and identity and culture, war and peace, love and life. I often sat in meetings, listening to managers drone on and on about the virtues of their company, trying to convince me to partner with them to bid a federal technology contract. When my mind wandered, a whistling came into my head, a familiar tune, many tunes, each one bringing me back to Dad, back to a special time and place of youth in Elko that mixed Basque customs, dance, language, sheep, cards, games of strength, and history.

In mid-phrase, he stopped. I noticed the absence.

"Santander!" Dad saw a sign overhead. "I been dere before. Small town, but good size."

"I thought you hadn't been along the coast."

"Only once for one day."

"When was that?"

"After I sell de Star Hotel, I come back here to see Momma and Daddy. I bought one car in Santander. It one French girl; I mean, French car."

"You bought a French girl, Dad?"

"I no say dat," he shot back testily.

"So you had a French girl in your car?"

"No, no."

"What was her name?"

"Dere no French girl."

"Was she Italian?" I laughed then.

"Dere no French girl, no girl. One French car. I mix up."

"I'm sure Freud would understand."

"What you mean?"

"Nothing."

"You shut up." He hit me in the arm.

The city of Santander had transitioned from the small, quaint seaside town that Dad had remembered to a burgeoning metropolis, the capital of Cantabria, with nearly 200,000 people. It felt like a tourist haven, congested with pedestrians and lines of cars speeding to the beach. I wondered from Dad's recollection if Santander had exchanged homespun distinction for sheer size, but the question remained unexplored as we made our way west along Spain's northern shore.

"We stop here?"

"Do you need a bathroom?"

"No. I good."

"Then we'll keep going."

"How far?"

"We'll drive until we run out of road," I said.

"We fall in de ocean."

"We'll stop before then."

Dad resumed whistling, picking up a different musical thread, touching old notes, and improvising around familiar melodies.

"Look at that," I said after a bend in the road overlooking a cove.

He straightened in his seat to focus on a bridge with white iron cables stretched in arcs to a cherry red base crossing a narrow waterway.

"What dey build dat for?"

"Looks like something from the Guggenheim in Bilbao."

"Ugly," Dad uttered, wrinkling his nose.

"You know what that reminds me of?" I asked him.

"One piece of shit?"

"No, Dad. That massive tree—that cement sculpture—between Elko and Salt Lake right in the middle of the desert. All you see for miles around—sagebrush, sagebrush, sagebrush—and then, a huge tree sculpture out of the blue."

"I seen dat."

"Well, it reminds me of that."

"One clear space, natural all 'round, but hell no, don' like dat, dey build one thing dere."

"We do that, don't we?"

"Damn right."

We didn't cross the bridge and didn't see others pass over it. I couldn't tell how a car reached it. I wondered if the country had built the bridge, like the

cement tree sculpture, to fill up space, or if it provided an important functional purpose. Seeing a replacement of nature's aesthetics with a stylized bridge reminiscent of the Guggenheim's modern architecture made me think that humans, even with efforts like the Guggenheim, still had a terrible time improving on nature.

Down a final winding road, we came to San Vicente. Already I sensed a remarkable beauty, not unlike that of the red clay roofs against the glowing green as we dipped over the last hill into Gernika's valley.

On the Iberian Peninsula, San Vicente lay halfway along the coast. The water was blue, a deep blue, like cobalt pottery fired in a kiln. The rolling hills were covered in tall grasses, green and lush but not dense like in Gernika, more wild than tame. All seemed clean and fresh, like a baby after a bath. In the cove, boats bobbed in the blue water, and each looked new and freshly painted, without barnacles or patches. San Vicente was an exclusive resort where boats had names, most likely after a lost love or child, as though the namesake could preserve the memory of the dearly departed. Everyone and everything exuded wealth here.

"Let's fin' de hotel."

"You tired?"

" 'bout dat time."

We checked in and were shown to a room with a view of the cove. The cost shocked me even though I had expected to be shocked.

"How much dis room?"

"Don't worry about it."

" 'spensive, huh?"

"Let's say we'll be eating a loaf of bread and water for dinner," I joked.

"Dat not bad."

I watched the tide recede as he slept. It went out fast and far without the moon's pull. Boats tilted to their sides on a white ocean floor scattered with shells and seaweed and sponges that missed their ride and perished under the hot sun. I marveled at its cleanliness—no bottles or debris, no signs of the trash or old tires so commonly strewn in the residue of low tides I had seen around the world. Here it reminded me again of Gernika and the fastidious marriage between nature and rare human tidiness.

I went out and curiously snooped about the town, climbed steep stairs to a castle that had once served as a fortified watchtower years before England had taken on the Armada and wrestled dominion of the sea from the Spanish.

It now served as the public government over San Vicente, but by the look of it, no one had bothered to show up for work except for a plump, well-groomed, kindly woman who sat reading a magazine at the front desk.

"Who works here?" I asked.

"All the government." She stood cordially and wiped her nose daintily with a tissue.

"The police and fire and the mayor, everyone?"

"Yes, but we have little need for them."

"Why is that?"

"No crime. Most everything works on its own."

"And taxes?"

"We have taxes, sure!" She rolled her eyes and gained volume with animation. "Too many taxes. But they go for everyone else in Spain. We support ourselves mostly." She softly pressed the tissue to her nose again.

I thanked her and went back out. From that higher perch, the town appeared stunningly beautiful, postcard perfect from every angle, and I believed then, as I do now, that had God constructed an Eden, He would have patterned it after San Vicente. Seldom had I felt remotely moved by natural wonders—Niagara, the Black Forest, Katrina, the Himalayas, and few others— but to the list I now added San Vicente, not for the breadth of falls or the height of mountains or the display of power, but merely for its peace and beauty, its combination of land and water and sky that the human eye instinctively recognized as supremely balanced even if the eye so rarely encountered it.

"Where you been?" Dad asked as I came into the room.

"Looking around. It's incredibly beautiful here."

"Lots of money, dough."

"I think you're right about that."

"Everyding beau'ful you got enough money."

"Probably some truth to that too."

Lying on the bed, I marveled at San Vicente's blessings of land and water and clean air. I recalled leading a delegation to America's Gulf Coast a year after Katrina's wrath. President George W. Bush had appointed me vice chairman of the AmeriCorps program in the United States, a volunteer role that took on unexpected dimensions after Katrina came ashore and thousands of our young AmeriCorps members deployed to Louisiana and Mississippi in the aftermath. During my visit, I talked with an African American

woman, plump and happy, nearly seventy years old, who hugged anyone within arm's reach. She cared for three grandchildren, each one skinny and spry and "a whole body full of trouble," she said. The hurricane had wiped out their home, but with the help of our members, she had recovered, she said, with a roof over her head, a bedroom for her grandchildren, and a small place for her. She seemed pleased and thankful. Shocking, I now thought, how two areas, seemingly equal in resources—water and air, rich culture and historic beauty—nonetheless housed people with extremely different accommodations and experiences in life.

Dad and I took the Subaru outside the town limits. The landscape remained untouched, pristine, as though protected perhaps by local ordinance to prevent development and growth. The town simply stopped along an imaginary line: inside the line—Eden with humans; outside the line—Eden without humans. It looked remarkably similar on both sides. I became hopeful that we monkeys could live symbiotically with nature without imprinting it too deeply, too permanently, but then again, I knew that San Vicente did not represent the vastness of humanity—poor, uneducated, less than dainty. It was a bubble with solid walls reinforced by a fortress of wealth and power.

———❦———

I wanted to stay another day in Eden, but our schedule and my diminished wallet kept us moving.

"Are you going to remember this place?"

"Yes—San Vicente—good name!"

"I will too," I replied.

We headed south away from the coast. The hills gained height and steepness as our Subaru rumbled slowly over each one only to start at the base of another.

"Dese damn hills, dey make me sick."

"Do you need to stop?"

"No, keepa goin'."

The base of every new hill—now mountain—started at a higher altitude than the last, so little by little, Dad and I ascended into the clouds and began to see snow, and a fog rolled off the ocean and settled in those early-morning hours before the sun climbed high enough to burn it off.

"I don' like dis."

"Don't like what?"

"Dis too high." He tightly gripped the handhold overhead. He squeezed so hard that his fingertips faded to white.

"We can't go any other way."

"What de name of dese fuckin' mountains?"

"They call them Los Picos de Europa—the Peaks of Europe. There's no bathroom around here, so I hope you went before we left."

"I go, but dis make my belly hurt."

"We can stop on the side if we need to."

"No, I don'. You know, Uncle Vicente, he tell me dat he drive one horse to Ok—how you say dat?"

"Say what?"

"It one state in Uni'ed Stets."

"There's fifty of them."

"You know—Oka."

"Oklahoma?"

"Yes, yes—Oklahoma."

"Uncle Vicente went to Oklahoma?"

"Yes, he did."

"Are you sure?"

"Dat's what he say."

"From Nevada?"

"Yes. Now you shut up," and he hit my arm.

"Go on," I said, still doubting that Uncle Vicente had traveled at some point across the North American continent to Oklahoma.

"He drive one horse to Oklahoma, and he eat beans or someding and he get sick in his stomach, and he have to stop. He go to de bushes, and he got no paper, so he pull up de grass to use. De grass it got—what you call dem—stickers, and den Uncle Vicente say he got stickers in his ass and he can't sit down for two weeks."

"Well, that's a nice story, Dad."

"It true." He laughed.

"Why did he go to Oklahoma?"

"Do it matter?"

"I'm curious why he drove a horse halfway across the country."

"Don' you listen to de story?"

"I did—the beans, the stickers, the painful ass—yes, I did. But I want to know why he went to Oklahoma on horseback all the way from Nevada."

"Don' matter. I can't 'splain it to you if you don' know."

"Fine."

The road narrowed as the rock face on our left became more jagged and the cliff on our right became more sheer.

"Look dat house." He pointed. "One crazy sonofabitch."

Around another bend, we saw a second and third, and then more, each appearing as though it had grown organically out of the hill's face rather than being constructed.

"They look impossible, just hanging there."

"I don' believe it."

"They're not that big, but I bet they cost an arm and leg to build."

"You right." He clutched the handhold harder, and I saw him tensing up.

"Calm down, Dad. We're not going to fall and we're almost to the top."

"I don' like dis."

"It seems some people do." The number of houses sprinkled and nestled among the trees and rocks had multiplied.

"Pretty soon, dis whole place be covered, next fifty or hundred years."

"Probably."

"Dey all look alike too."

Each one, suspended from steel rods bolted to the mountain, had a white or brown frame, probably two bedrooms, though impossible to say how deeply it recessed underground. For all I knew, the facade hid a vast network that extended for miles beneath the surface, but I doubted that.

"Why dey live dere?"

"I don't know. Probably to keep up with the Joneses."

"What?"

"There's an old saying that neighbors try to keep up with neighbors, what they call the Joneses. If the Joneses next door get a new car, then the people next to them need a new car. If the Joneses get a boat, then their neighbor needs a boat. It doesn't matter if they can afford it. After one person built a house here on the mountain, someone else saw that and decided to do the same thing. Pretty soon, more people will see it and then—you're right—in fifty or a hundred years, there's going to be houses all along here. By then, they might have an elevator so you won't have to hold so hard to that handle."

"I not holdin' hard."

"Looks like all the blood's gone from your hands." He pulled them down self-consciously.

"Dey protect dis like Lamoille Canyon. Dey protect Lamoille, don't dey?" he asked, referring to the forested area outside of Elko.

"They do, and you hope they would protect this too, but when you have more and more people, and they all need a place to live and see this unused land, before you know it, the laws change. The government says, 'We'll just take a mile off the ends and leave the rest,' and in a few more years, they take another mile and another and another until pretty soon not much is protected anymore."

"Dat's where it headin', anyway."

"Why do you think that?"

"Too many people. It don' happen here only. Dat happen everywhere."

"Probably so, Dad."

Dad's prediction took me back ten years to a cross-country trip that he and I had made from Nevada to Virginia. After leaving office with Governor Miller's administration, I started up the East Coast branch of a technology company out of my back bedroom. Dad and I drove a southern route, passing from small town to small town, trying to avoid large cities. We hoped to absorb the richness of local customs, architectures, accents, and people. What we discovered instead was that each town looked very much like the next one in line, heavily influenced, even overwhelmed by Walmarts, Starbucks, Home Depots, Targets, McDonald's, Pizza Huts, and an assortment of others. Rarely did we discern anything new and fresh and different across nearly 2,500 miles of travel. I wondered if all towns and countries, including Euskadi, awaited a similar destiny. I thought Dad had already decided, but I remained hopeful that the reclusiveness of his generation might still hold some sway.

Our lumbering Subaru grunted and groaned to the summit. We pulled over to see a broad panorama of Los Picos de Europa, which stretched endlessly in a pattern of peak, valley, peak, valley in nearly perfect succession like an EKG of the planet. The cold air smelled of sweet pine, and spots of water spewed— not like falls, more like slow runoff—down rock walls in the distance.

Dad peed off the edge as I rummaged in the Subaru for a loaf of French bread, meats, and cheeses. We made sandwiches sitting on a log looking over the scene and ate lunch without a car or a bird or a single sound to disturb us.

In a hundred years, no one would believe this moment of sanctuary could have happened.

Tipping over the summit, we gradually descended into a softer valley. The Subaru breathed relief, the air warmed, and the road widened. Dad no longer gripped the handhold, though he had left a permanent imprint, and his blood pressure fell.

In a window of twenty miles, trees at altitude gave way to tall grasses and small ponds and then larger ponds, not a swamp but a wet flatness where reeds and bamboo might have found a hospitable home. And then the window closed. The wetness dried instantly into a savannah, as though nature herself had watched our progress and squeezed more and more water from the land with every mile we traveled south.

"Amazing isn't it, Dad?"

"What dat?"

"Twenty miles back we were in the mountains—hard to live there. Then we go twenty miles down and it turns into this dried-up grassland—also hard to live here."

"People, dey find a way. If dere's noding else, dey live anywhere. Den everyding, it get swallowed up. No one, dey live 'lone after dat."

A sign on the road read PALENCIA.

"That's where we're staying."

"Down here?"

"Just a little farther."

"Dat's good. I need one nap."

## 10

After Dad and Mom married, he bought the Blue Jay Bar across the tracks about two hundred feet from the Star Hotel. He built a small apartment in the back with two bedrooms, bathroom, and kitchen, fraying carpet, worn furniture, and a black-and-white television with nonfunctioning rabbit ears. Anything used and tattered, Mom made spotless and comfortable.

A small doorway separated the apartment from the bar, which smelled of either Pine-Sol and Clorox or beer. No other odors penetrated these olfactory extremes.

Patrons came in by 11 AM, some staying for an hour until lunch, and others remaining until the 9 PM closing. What the regulars lacked in number, they made up for in predictability, taking a day off a year—Christmas—not because the bar closed, or because they held the day sacred, but because spiked eggnog flowed freer and more abundantly in their own homes or at a neighbor's party than it ever could in our bar. The regulars were creatures of habit who sought drink of least resistance.

Jack, a retired teacher and a regular, had taught high school writing and literature for thirty years, serving as one of the best, most thoughtful educators who had ever graced the English department of our small town, or so I had been told. He liked highballs with little water, or whiskey straight, one shot every couple of hours, with conversation and argument filling the void between swigs. His blond hair lay like straw and his bloodshot eyes sagged. He drank more than most, but rarely exhibited slurred speech, imbalanced swagger, or sleepiness. He had a soft demeanor and made people feel safe, though every instinct told them to steer clear of men who drowned their own livers.

When I turned four, Dad galloped from one end of the bar to the other with me on his back. My little hands lost their grip around his burly neck, and as I began to fall, he caught my arm from behind and snapped it in three places. Mom hurried me to the emergency room, where Dr. Moren, the same doctor who had delivered me, x-rayed my arm and molded a cast from hand to elbow.

When I returned to the bar, Jack pulled a pen from his breast pocket and signed the pristine, still-drying plaster—*Little man, hurt arm, dry your tears, stay from harm, be strong, go far, little man, hurt arm.*

Mom liked the verse so much she had me show it to everyone. Juanito saw the scribbles but couldn't read them. He smiled and cradled my small arm in his hands and said, "Priddy nice." A sheepherder who boarded at the Star, he commanded only a handful of English words. He was diminutive in size and appeared quiet and unassuming, but if struck by something funny, he exploded with a hyena laugh, part hiccup, part wheeze. People around him laughed too, not with him but in spite of him, as though Juanito's cackle showed God's own sense of humor on display.

Not able to write himself, Juanito sketched next to Jack's lines a caricature of a buxom woman wearing a miniskirt, hands on her knees and bent over with a suggestive smile. Then came his airy laugh as he recapped the pen. Forbidden artistry compensated for his lack of language.

Mom came around the bar in full-protection mode to see the picture.

With hands on hips and a towel tossed over her shoulder, she angrily yelled, "Juanito, get out."

"What I do?" he said, still laughing.

"You know what you did. Get out now." And Juanito left.

With a black marker, Mom scribbled out the erotic character, erasing part of Jack's poetic verse with it.

Juanito returned the next day, as if the incident had not occurred, though Mom still carried a little maternal contempt. More than a regular, Juanito played *mus* at the corner card table with other Basque sheepherders.

The game put poker to shame. Played with a partner, *mus* excluded eights, nines, and tens from a regular deck, included four games in one, and used special signals to communicate with a partner—biting a lower lip, winking the left eye, raising eyebrows, scowling with half the mouth, or poking the tongue between the teeth. Watching old-timers play left an impression of clever men with facial tics fiercely competing for something more than chips.

Another connoisseur of the game, Chapo, was round in every way—round head, round belly, round eyes, rounded teeth, at least those still intact. Only five feet two inches, this small-statured man was underestimated by many, leaving them vulnerable to his wily cleverness hidden just beneath his happy smile. Chapo won most of his *mus* games. Some argued that in addition to the regular signals, he used coded sips of wine or whiskey, or encrypted blinks and throat clearings, though no one charged anything beyond suspicion. With such complexity, the clever could overwhelm the feeble without revealing any obvious deceptions. In truth, Chapo mastered the subtle human dimensions of each match, winning far more than he ever lost and representing Elko at regional, national, and international competitions.

Castillo, on the other hand, rarely won a match. *Mus* was not his gift. He was an older, balding, white-haired man, who had retired from sheepherding and now spent his days in the Blue Jay drinking wine and talking with a happy spirit. His gift was an ability to connect with people. Standing six inches taller than most others, he remained warm and gentle, like a happy giant, and pulled people in around him. As business picked up, Dad hired Castillo as backup bartender, and seeing him every day turned him from a bartender into a part of the family, a surrogate uncle, whom I called Cico (*Kee*-koe), because I couldn't pronounce his full name. Over time, the nickname stuck and most everyone in the bar adopted it.

Each afternoon, I made my way from our apartment to the bar counter, where I knew Cico would be indulging a wonderful habit. He scooped ice cream from the cooler, mixed it until it was soft like a milk shake, and then drank it from the bowl. If he saw me coming, he slurped faster to avoid sharing while I pulled my four-year-old body on a stool to face him.

"Can I have some?" I'd ask.

"You don't tell your daddy." He raised a finger at me.

I repeated, "Can I have some?"

He let me dip a finger in the bowl or sip the sweet concoction that he sometimes swirled with chocolate syrup. These sugary slurps were hush money. I knew that, and so did Cico. I didn't tell Dad about them, though he or Mom might have suspected from Cico's swelling belly.

Mom forbade me to sit at the bar counter. She thought it improper for children. When she went on errands while Dad napped, I quietly made my way to the bar floor, admired the mugs, shot glasses, and thin-necked wineglasses stacked in pyramids, and felt mesmerized by the back-to-back mirrors that bounced reflections of reflections back and forth, producing smaller and smaller images until they seemed to disappear down a tunnel.

From behind the barstools, I played my favorite game—*I'm-in-prison*. I ran around the pool table, rolled the cue ball, or hid underneath. I indulged these luxuries only when Cico tended bar. Other times Mom or Dad shooed me back to the apartment, where I watched one of two snowy channels on our black-and-white television or set up tents with couch cushions and blankets.

Outside the bar, we had a yard enclosed by a chain-link fence, but Mom did not want me to play there unless supervised. The Blue Jay sat behind the Stockmen's Hotel, between two railroads, one fifty feet from the door of our apartment and the other two blocks north, running through the middle of town. Mom feared that drunkards from the Stockmen's or hobos who passed by train might lie in wait to snatch me up and carry me away. Her reasoning scared me, probably to good effect.

I left the Blue Jay only under rare circumstances. Whenever Dad needed a haircut, he assumed I needed one too. He would take me by the hand and together we would cross the tracks to Julio's barbershop. I wanted to put a penny on the track, hoping the train might come and smear it, but Mom said that doing so could inadvertently derail the train or accidentally pull me under. Dad didn't mind, but he had no time for it, so in all those years of haircuts at Julio's, I never smeared a penny on the track.

Julio was among the oldest of Basque men. He had ended his sheepherding career decades before and had then taken up comb and scissors to become the town's premier barber for Basque men and boys. The shop smelled of tobacco and Aqua Velva. Between his lips, he chewed a cigar, an inch long and soggy, as if he had started it at full length and little by little had gnawed the casing and swallowed it bit by bit. His words slurred, encumbered by his eighty years; his eyesight was diminished, if not gone; and his hands shook just like my grandmother's, a condition I later learned was called Parkinson's. A snip here, another there, and by the end, my bangs trended diagonal, my part slanted, and I held a tissue on both ears to stanch the bleeding. Dad paid Julio $1.50 for the cut.

"Don' tell your mama we come here," Dad said on our way back.

"I promise. Cross my heart," and I crossed it with a finger.

It didn't occur to either of us that our mutual secret lay in the open.

Mom hurried around the bar as we came in.

"Damn it, Joe, his head looks like a rooster's ass," she said. One hand went to her hip and the other whipped him with a dish towel.

"It's fine," he said.

"It's not fine," she yelled back. "If you want your head to look like a rooster's ass, that's fine, but don't do it to him. Do you hear me? Don't take him there again. I mean it."

She had given this command several times, but once her anger simmered down and my hair grew out, she forgot about it.

Had Dad and I walked one block beyond Julio's, near the Humboldt River along Third Street, we would have come to Elko's brothels—Inez's, Mona's, PJ's, and Sue's. Only rumors spoke of their clientele. The establishments supposedly catered to sheepherders during the off season, gold miners surrounding Elko County, and a handful of allegedly upstanding, highly respected residents of the community.

Naturally, no one confirmed any firsthand knowledge of Elko's brothels. In fact, such sins seemed immaculately conducted without sinners. But these houses operated year after year with little regard for the boom-and-bust cycles of the gold mining industry, economic downturn in the state, or any national recession. They had paying customers, anonymous, but frequent enough that they could stay in business and turn a profit. The workers at the brothels blended into town life, shopped at grocery stores, attended Little

League games, and even went to church. They did not signal their occupation in public through conspicuous attire as prostitutes who walk boulevards. As citizens, they worked and paid taxes, and like their clientele, kept a low profile to avoid questions and judgment.

Mom and Dad did not speak of Elko's cathouses directly. Anything beyond Julio's was spoken of with dark, hushed tones of evil and danger.

"Children drown down by the river," Mom would say.

"What children?" I would ask, as if the Humboldt sensed a presence, swelled from its banks, and devoured children who ventured too close.

"You might know them. I don't know," she'd say to scare me.

Then she'd start another line of protective trepidation.

"A child got kidnapped down there," she would say, pointing to Third Street.

"What child? Who kidnapped them?"

Not answering, she would respond, "So you never want to go down there, not even with an adult. You hear me?"

"Yes," I responded as much in obedience as in fear.

*Not even with an adult* put the exclamation on the point. Such over-whelming and hideous treachery lay in wait down Third Street that even adults were not safe. Mom's warnings dropped fear like an anvil on me and kept me firmly planted at the Blue Jay. Whatever shadows lurked by the Humboldt remained monsters of my mind, caged and confined, not to be released. Mom did her job well.

If Dad took me one block south to Julio's, Mom took me one block north to Puccinelli's Market, or more specifically, Puccinelli's Butcher Shop. It stood next to the post office and smelled of sausage and chorizo with a layer of saw-dust on the floor to soak up blood and goo that dripped from meat cuttings.

As much as Third Street darkly bedeviled my imagination, Angelo Puccinelli paralyzed me. He was a thin, tall Italian man with a gruff, loud, intimidating voice that exploded from a narrow face framed by long sideburns. He wore an apron turned red with blood spatters. In his right hand, like a natural exten-sion of his arm, he wielded a sharpened meat axe to part ribs and carve steak. I imagined it cleaving open a skull just as easily. Mom called Angelo a nice man without an inside voice. But he still made me quake in my little shoes, and I much preferred facing Julio's scissors than Angelo's axe.

If not at Puccinelli's, Mom took me to pick up Jonna from Southside Ele-mentary, the same school that I would attend when I reached kindergarten age in another year. While home alone, I occupied my time as best I could, but on weekends and during the summer months, my opportunities for play expanded because of Jonna's exploits.

She and I once collected rocks from the backyard and washed them with soap. In front of the Blue Jay, we set up a card table, marked the rocks with a price, no more than ten cents each, and sold them to bar patrons who happened by. I didn't think we'd sell a single rock, since anyone with half a brain could pick one up for free out of the gutter. But surprisingly, everyone who passed bought more than one. Then before going inside, they chucked the rocks to the street. When the door shut behind them, Jonna ordered me to go get the rocks so we could resell them.

Our little business thrived for an hour, until Dad came out and made us pack up. One of his customers had said, jokingly, that all his money had gone for rocks and he had none left for beer. With a 100 percent margin, we tried to convince Dad to give up selling beer in favor of rocks—but no sell.

Jonna and I shared a room, each of us with a single bed separated by dresser drawers without rollers and missing knobs. We had to pull with four hands to open them. We set a rule not to close the drawers all the way, though Mom came around every morning, all neat and tidy, and shut them, leaving us to tackle the knobless beast that trapped our clothes and socks.

On my fifth birthday, I woke to find a tricycle wrapped in a blue bow, glistening cherry red with reflective chrome and white tassels hanging from the handlebars. It glowed as a spectacle, a thing of radiance that left me chattering and gleeful, wound up with energy, beaming and proud, and aching to hop on and take it for a spin.

Mom carried it to the bar, where a wide, tiled floor opened up like a racetrack. I had endless visions of pedaling hither and thither, circling the pool table, and slamming into stools. Every vision awaited action.

As Mom set my new tricycle down, Jonna burst from nowhere, hopped on, and took off. Shocked and hurt, I cried, immediately thinking it my gift not hers, my birthday not hers. Mom yelled, but Jonna pedaled back only when ready.

I quickly dried my tears, climbed aboard, and swirled faster and faster around the pool table. After two or three laps, Jonna asked me to stop and allow her to stand on the red step in the back and place her hands on my shoulders. My little legs pressed hard to carry the extra weight. Gaining momentum, we hurtled around the pool table again as her bony knees poked into my fleshy back. I heard a piercing scream very near my ear: "Pedal faster. Pedal faster."

When closing came, well past bedtime, odors of spilt beer and human sweat wafted through the apartment. I wandered out of bed into the bar as neon flickered and smells of Pine-Sol and Clorox burned my nose and eyes. I saw Dad pushing a mop, exerting his rounded back. He had been up for eighteen hours, cleaning counters and washing glasses, carrying cases of beer and wine from the cellar, and tending to customers. Sweat dripped down his cheeks. How those shoulders ached, how those forearms burned, how those legs wobbled and groaned for sleep. That silhouette in dim light became a permanent fixture in my mind's eye, remaining unalterable and immune to the debilitating effects of time on flesh and bone.

When Dad caught me watching, he finished his work and blew his nose, making me giggle, and then scooped me up in his hairy arms, all wet and smelling of salt. He took an upturned stool off the bar, poured a glass of wine, and lit a Winston, bouncing me on his knee. We sat silently in a room that an hour before had bustled with raucous drunkards.

"You want sip?" he asked.

I nodded and he held the glass to my lips.

I coughed and spit it out and scraped my tongue with my hand.

He laughed.

He whistled melodies from ancient Basque songs between cigarette puffs as echoes fell like fairy dust on our ears. He downed the last drops of his wine and then carried me to bed, tucking me under the covers and kissing me good night.

Many years later, I served as an advisor to then Governor Miller in Nevada, forming policy and shepherding legislation on health care, education, and technology. During a panel discussion one day on drug abuse, an expert witness argued in favor of punishing parents who gave beer and alcohol to young children. I conjured the memory of sitting on Dad's lap during those lonely nights at the Blue Jay so many years before. I asked the expert, "Even a sip?" and he replied, "Any amount, even a sip." As a teetotaler, I caught myself laughing out loud, but asked no more questions of him or others, though I knew that punishing someone like Dad offered zero chance of solving drug abuse problems. Unbeknownst to him, the expert's fight quietly ended that day.

These memories carried into my dreams, twisting as I slept. Monsters rode tricycles from Third Street; butchers followed with scissors, not axes; trains shook the house and then derailed from a misplaced penny; Juanito laughed and Jack told stories; men threw cards and tossed rocks; and pool tables filled with an infinite number of balls.

My dreams morphed night after night, reflecting my very little world. A year later, Dad and Mom bought a sheep farm up a crooked road on Elko's outskirts. It became the place I remember most and where I learned to dream anew.

## 11

The high-altitude romp through Los Picos de Europa had drained Dad. After arriving in Palencia, we ate an early dinner while watching Barcelona trounce a foreign team 4–0 in a televised soccer match. The meal took three hours as we waited for the cook, dishwasher, and waiter to get their fill of highlights throughout the evening. Afterward, Dad limped to the room on a bad hip and turned in by 8 PM. He slept the night, not waking for the bathroom or to check his surroundings.

"When you getting up?" Dad poked and roused me from sleep. I had slept through his early-morning nose blowing.

"What time is it?"

"Eight o'clock." A dim light pierced the curtains. Looking at my watch, I saw 6:15 AM. Dad often exaggerated the lateness of the hour whenever he wanted to go somewhere. He had already dressed in one of his two pairs of jeans and a shirt he had worn two days before.

"Your belly's getting big," I said, noticing the waistband turned outward.

"No. Dis damn belt getting too small."

"Yeah, that's the problem."

I pulled clothes from my bag and showered as he clicked through channels on the television. He didn't stop two seconds in any one place.

In the car, I arranged the GPS and scanned a map from the front desk.

"Where we goin' today?" he asked.

"Is there any place you want to go?"

"Don' care. I don' know noding here."

"I thought we'd see a couple places."

"Dat's good."

The city of Palencia, lying in the central lowlands away from the northern coast, had more than 80,000 people. Through the center, the Carrion River carved the city in half—on the left side were old structures dating to the city's origin, demonstrating stone and architecture centuries old, and on the other side were residential neighborhoods. The town melded old and new without appearing disjointed or sacrificing a rich heritage of ecclesiastical tradition and medieval architecture.

Unlike the crowded towns smashed between ocean and mountain along the coast, here the roads opened wider, on flatter land, and breathing felt easier and claustrophobia less a concern. The British female GPS voice took us straight away without hairpin turns or single-lane avenues fitting two lanes of cars.

"What de hell is dat?"

"They call that El Cristo del Otero, Dad."

"Dat's one statue of Jesus Christ?"

"Yes, but probably not an exact replica." I smirked sarcastically.

"How dey build dat?"

"With a lot of patience and a great deal of cement."

We wound the Subaru around, drawing closer to the base where Christ's big toe protruded from under a long robe. El Cristo stood nearly a hundred feet high, with arms outstretched, open palms in front blessing the town. A similar statue in Rio de Janeiro inched out Palencia's as the world's tallest replica of Christ. As we rose higher and higher, Dad gripped the seat belt and the handhold where he had left a permanent imprint from our trek through Los Picos de Europa.

"Dis high enough," he said.

"Just a little more, Dad. We're not going to fall."

"How you know?"

"Because I'm driving. Have a little faith. I'm not Amy." My younger sister had wrecked nearly every car she had driven.

"Your sister, she a good driver," he said in defense. "She go a little fast, but you don' tell her I say dat."

At the base, Dad and I snapped pictures vertically to capture the grandiosity of El Cristo. The elongated facial features atop a lengthy robe added illusion to the statue's true height. A blue sky of wispy clouds surrounded the stone with a heavenly impression. From the platform, we viewed Palencia, a panorama of savannah grasses, a river through the middle, and churches that dwarfed all other human or natural creations.

"Look at that," I said with a gasp.

"Dry. I didn't know dis country got dry land like dat."

"That's because you only lived by the ocean."

"Dis look like Elko."

"Not quite. No sagebrush. What do you think of this?" I thumbed at El Cristo behind us.

"Bah!"

"What do you mean, 'Bah!'? It's one of the largest statues in the world."

"I don't know why dey build dis, waste of money."

"I suppose they built it to honor Christ."

"If you don' wear no shoes, you don' need no statues." He pointed to Christ's bare feet.

"You're probably right. But you told me that you sold bread in Lekeitio under that crucifix there."

"Dat's right. Away from de soldiers. Dey don' boder you dere."

"I bet you were glad the statue was there then."

"No one selling bread here. No soldiers either."

"I mean that it served a purpose for you—different things for different people."

"What purpose? Jesus Cristo," he said, "He can't afford no shoes. He don' want no statue neither."

"What do you think He wants?"

"To be good, dat's all. Be good to each oder."

We sat on a rock admiring the full swath of Palencia and noticing with each survey a new landmark or point of interest. An hour passed, and the noon sun beamed, making our perch uncomfortable.

"Let's go," Dad said. He got up. "Ay! Ay! My back."

"Oh, for heaven's sake, Dad. Where do you want to go?"

"You de driver."

"You want to eat?"

"No, not me."

"Are you sure?" I knew different.

He half smiled as if caught in a fib and said, "Okay, let's eat."

He ate a local favorite—*lechazo*—a meat from a baby lamb that had drunk only its mother's milk. It flaked tenderly from the bone.

"You know, Dad, there's a group in the United States that wouldn't like you eating that."

"Group? What group?" he said with a hint of disdain.

"They call it PETA."

"PETA? Dat some bread, no?"

"Doesn't matter," I said, paying the bill and getting ready to leave.

"Where to now?" he asked.

"We're going to see a church."

"A church? What de hell for?"

"It's not any church. It's Palencia's cathedral; it's one of the biggest in the world."

"Bah!"

"Just get in the damn car."

Following the GPS, our Subaru crawled into the old part of Palencia, through narrow streets lined with miniature shops displaying antique metal bowls and water pitchers, incense burners, and crosses and crucifixes of varying sizes and composition—ivory, obsidian, wood—some laden with jewels, others solid gold or silver. Ten blocks ahead, a structure rose with Gothic majesty and permanence, growing impossibly larger as we approached.

Outside its three-story vaulted doors, the Cathedral of Palencia seemed equally tall and broad. After eighty-three years of construction, beginning in 1321, it gained prominence as a chief center of the Inquisition during the reign of Isabella and Ferdinand, who, more than any other regal pair, unified Spain as a Catholic monarchy. Buried beneath was Saint Antoninus of Pamiers (San Antolin), on whose hallowed, blessed remains, from sacred bone and blood, the church traced its divine right as a legitimate house of God.

Inside, Dad and I pressed our fingers in holy water and made the sign of the cross.

"Which way we go?" he asked. His voice echoed in the exalted ceilings.

"Talk quieter. Did you learn to whisper in a barn?"

"I think I did," he said.

At the end of a long stone corridor with crypts and portraits on either side, we stopped at a retable of stunning gold. Separate chapels showed biblical images—Mary and Joseph, John and Peter and Paul, Jesus in His mother's lap or bearing sin on the cross. I recognized a few. A light shining from each side reflected a resplendent brightness.

"What do you think of that?" I chirped in Dad's ear.

"Lots of gold," he said. His voice bumped around in the ceiling and came back to us as echo.

In a pew nearby, a kneeling woman running fingers over a Rosary shushed us. We moved on.

In the sacristy, a painting, *St. Sebastian,* by El Greco, caught my eye.

"You see this?"

"Yes, one painting."

"That guy is Saint Sebastian."

"He got one arrow dere. Why don' he pull it out?" Dad's little half laugh resonated stronger than his whispers.

"They say that his wife couldn't speak, not for many years, but one day he touched her lips with his hand, made the sign of the cross, and forever more, she could speak."

"Bullshit!" The word turned pious heads throughout the cathedral. Not waiting for anyone else to do so, I shushed Dad myself.

"They said that he cured diseases when he baptized people."

"Do he fix gout in my big toe?" he whispered.

"That arrow in his side came from when he was a soldier. The Romans found out he was Christian and shot him, not with one arrow but many. He lived, even though he lost a great deal of blood. After he healed, he told his story as a miracle and turned a lot of people into Christians."

"So dey make him one saint?"

"That's right."

"Lots of nonsense." Several shushes came from different directions.

"I'm just telling you the story, Dad."

Sensing that a gang of shushers had begun to mount, and we might have been moments away from resurrecting the Inquisition, I decided an early departure seemed wise.

"Let's go out here, Dad."

Outside we sat on a bench in a mostly deserted courtyard with handfuls of nuns and priests walking, hands folded, with a purposeful stride. Above on each of the cathedral's corners, gargoyles watched over us.

"Do you need a nap?"

"Pretty soon."

"What'd you think?"

"Bah!"

"Come on, it's one of the oldest, biggest churches in the world."

"See if you understand me. Dis all fine . . . good . . ." He exaggerated the length of the words. "One big building, one big church." His arms flailed to emphasize size. "But dat don' mean noding," he said, pointing to the cathedral. "You make one building bigger, dat don' make faith bigger."

I nodded.

"You know, when I herdin' sheep, I don' have no church or no statues or no paintings. I don' have shit. But every day, every day"—he raised his finger for emphasis—"I have faith and I say one prayer."

"What'd you pray about?"

"I pray sheep be safe, not to lose one, or dat I don' get one snowstorm. I pray dat I see Momma and Daddy and sisters and brother again. Dose prayers, dey de ones dat matter. Dey simple."

"You don't go to church either."

"Dat's right, I don'. But you don' need no church. All dis shit, and dat boy with one arrow, dat don' mean noding. Dat statue we seen dis morning, it don' mean noding. Faith, you have it here." He touched his chest.

"Dere's lots of people. See if you understand me. Dey go to church every Sunday, some go every day, and dey do bad things. Lots of people never go and dey de best people. Go—don't go—Be one good person—dat's what Christ He want."

"I thought you believed God knew everything."

"He know what in de heart."

"Doesn't He know what you're up to every minute?"

"Maybe He know. Maybe He don' care."

"I thought He kept our name in His book."

"Maybe He do dat. I don' know."

"You don't know?"

"Nobody know dat. Just be good person, dat's all, and do good, not say good."

When Dad said that, I thought of the two boys confronted in the field by their father. The father asked the first boy, "Will you help me in the vineyard?"

The boy responded, "No," but grudgingly acquiesced and did the work.

The father asked the second boy the same thing.

He responded, "Certainly, I will go, sir," but then the boy stayed away to avoid the work.

Which boy did the will of his father?

Some said the second. To do a day's work was not significant, but to say "No" to one's father was a grievous sin.

I thought differently. Actions, not words, showed obedience to one's father. Deeds dictated true devotion, kindness, and love. Speaking His words meant very little without wearing His shoes and walking His path.

"You know, Dad—see if you understand me," I said sarcastically, "I read a story once about a guy who comes to Seville here in Spain. You don't know who the guy is; he doesn't say a word. But when he comes to town, he sees a blind man and makes him see. He sees a small girl in a coffin with flowers, and he makes her rise up and live again. He sees people with diseases and cures them."

"Dat Jesus Christ."

"You don't know that in the story."

"Who else it could be?"

"Maybe nobody else, but you don't know that. What happens is that the cardinal comes and has the soldiers arrest the man and throw him in jail."

"He put Jesus Cristo in jail?"

"That's right, or whoever the guy is. Remember, he doesn't say a word, so you don't know for sure. But the cardinal goes to the jail to talk to him. He tells him that the people can't stand his trickery. It confuses them, he says. He tells the guy that the church is more important because it gives people bread, and that without the church, people wouldn't know what to do or how to make decisions. He tells him that the church from time to time gives people miracles that they can believe in and hope for and pray over. Without all of that, he told him, the people would fall apart and not know what to do with their lives."

"I don' believe dat. I don' go to church, and I do all right."

"I know you do. I'm just telling the story."

"So what de cardinal he do?"

"He lets the guy go. He opens up the jail and sends him away and tells him not to come back ever again, so without saying a word, the man leaves the jail, walks out the door, and never returns."

"I don' like dat."

"I didn't think you would."

Smiling at him, I asked, "Are you ready for a nap?"

"I dink so," he said.

We rose from our bench in the courtyard. Walking to the car, we intersected with a nun dressed in a habit with the hood pulled so tight that it stretched her cheeks, squinted her eyes, and warped her forehead.

" 'Scuse me," Dad said, stopping to let her pass.

The nun scowled and moved past us.

# 12

Ana Mari Arbillaga stood with her back to us, arms raised, fingers snapping. During her workday, she cooked at the Nevada Dinner House, one of three Basque restaurants in Elko, and then on weekends she turned into the patron saint of Elko's Basque heritage—dance instructor, seamstress, Basque-to-English translator, and letter writer. If the Basques had a matriarch in Elko, Ana Mari qualified. She talked like Dad, conveying more meaning with inflection, volume, and hand gestures than with words.

"Toe-heel-toe-kick. Now de oder foot," she said.

Then we repeated, "Toe-heel-toe-kick."

"Now go side to side," and we obeyed.

Twenty of us little Basque urchins stood in a single row behind her. She had a black, wiry bob-cut hairdo, a Roman nose, droopy eyes, and thin, lanky legs. In imitation, we held our arms over our heads, watched her feet, and parroted her moves. The snapping fingers came later. Our dexterity was limited.

Toe-heel-toe-kick.

Toe-heel-toe-kick.

We started with our right foot, then repeated the same four moves with our left until we twirled with the transition of the music. Following the spin, we did a dreaded side-to-side maneuver. Our sneakers squealed on the lacquered wooden floor.

"Lef' to right first," Ana Mari said.

If she had to say it more than once, her gentleness disappeared and she spit, "Lef' to right first. Lef' to right. Stupido."

Not all of us learned the lesson, not even after repeated bumps, collisions, and a few floor flops. Oh, these were happy, clumsy times, a full immersion in Basque culture beyond the *mus* games and sheepherders of the Blue Jay Bar.

"Dis is de jota," Ana Mari described.

So few Basque youngsters had an obvious rhythmical gift for dance that I wondered how it had become a hallmark of our ethnic identity. We danced as we might stomp ants, and though we learned the steps—many steps to many dances—some of us became nothing more than highly adept ant stompers.

A few standouts graced the lacquered floor. Ricardo and Stephanie, a brother and sister duo, took on nearly mythical stature. Their feet flashed with not a squeal of rubber sole, only staccato toe taps and flamboyant kicks and artful flowing twirls as Goya might paint them. Their feet flew while their torsos remained still. I thought the two of them to be as well known around the country as in Elko, evidence of the smallness of my world.

Every week on Saturday afternoon, Mom dropped me and Jonna at the Girl Scout House, a building with bright green trim that never faded no matter how hot the summer or how cold the winter. Across the street was Ernie Hall Baseball Diamond, named for a local benefactor and longtime resident who loved the game. Behind the Scout House lived my best friend, Mikel, who, like me, struggled to master Ana Mari's lessons.

Inside during practices, Bernardo—Ricardo and Stephanie's father—played the accordion and Gene joined on the clarinet. Bernardo and Gene did not read music. They played by ear in a type of unified improvisation week after week, as Basque tadpoles like me and Mikel toed and heeled and toed and kicked our way through each painful, inept, inelegant step. Bernardo's fingers flew over his vertical keyboard, and Gene maneuvered elegantly up and down the treble staff. They knew a hundred songs or more, played nonstop at our practices, during the festival in July, and at public and private parties. No one asked who had taught them or how they'd learned. We only knew that Bernardo and Gene became the bright and buoyant sound of our Basque ancestry.

Mikel and I became friends at these practices and, over time, best friends—inseparable. Both of us had timid demeanors and enjoyed quiet. Others preferred loud and boisterous—Jose and Fermin, Ana Mari's sons; the Samper brothers, Marcus and Jerome; two of the Echeverrias, Tim and Matt; and select others who, in any given week, ran the gamut between sedate and unruly. A week did not pass that a member of the "Big Group," as they were called, did not tease, torment, trample, or threaten any member of the "Young Group," as we were called.

Mikel and I avoided Big Group encroachments by watching them dance from afar or allowing them to enter or leave the building first. We kept a healthy distance from them. We had nearly equal dancing prowess—or rather, no dancing prowess whatsoever. Our bond arose from a common commiseration about our weekly stumbles and bumbles and fears of public humiliation. Enduring a great suffering drew people together.

After Ana Mari's toe-heel-toe-kick, we advanced to the *porrusalda,* an equally perilous sequence of fancy footwork. Someone somewhere named it after leek soup, a watery appetizer without an ounce of flavor, and in this case, a proper metaphor for my dancing style.

"Lef' forward, den back," Ana Mari gently told us urchins. "Now, right forward, den back."

And when many of us confused right with left, she put away gentleness to yell, "No! No! Lef'! Lef'! Stupido. Now right."

Grasping the binary footwork, we still struggled with technique and finesse. "No shuffle, shuffle. You put de toes forward. Don' clean de floor," she said.

But shuffles came from my feet and from Mikel's and in our two spots, more than in others, the floor glowed with a bright sheen.

Once learned, the *porrusalda* joined to the *jota* like a second movement of an unending symphony. The pairing lasted an eternity and prompted rolling thoughts of denial—these feet don't belong to me; they don't follow my commands; I can't be held responsible; is amputation possible?

My foot skill maxed out after the *jota* and the *porrusalda*. Neurons fired, but conductivity from head to toe moved at a snail's pace. Other dancers had built a vast repertoire of ten or fifteen dances, and had closed the gap with Stephanie and Ricardo's obvious grace and talent, although everyone knew they still held a comfortable edge. You can't put in what God's left out. Mikel fared little better than me, but even he pulled ahead. I had flatlined. Everyone recognized my deficiencies. Ana Mari casually told me, "You sit down o' you get hurt."

Despite my three left feet, the dances left me enamored of the intricate richness of steps, snapping fingers, twirling bodies, and the more advanced scissor-jumps and knee-to-nose high kicks. No one encouraged me to twist my legs to mimic scissors or touch my knee to my nose. Naturally, they cared about my safety. But Ana Mari pulled me—reluctantly—into another dance, one that relied more on arms and not feet.

Two lines of guys, carrying a three-foot stick in each hand, filed like miniature soldiers onto the floor. Bernardo and Gene started playing. I turned inward to face Mikel and I struck my stick with his in a cracking cadence. Then I turned to the guy at my side and repeated the sequence.

As in the *jota* and the *porrusalda*, I claimed no great talent, but fortunately, the dance gods demanded little skill and even less precision for the stick dance. For once the ungifted thrived. If I missed a strike and hit myself or someone else, it wasn't confirmable unless one of us stopped to rub his forehead or temple. None of us would do that, lest we betray an instinctive masculinity. Each strike grew harder than the last until needles shot into our hands and up our arms and made our shoulders ache. As Bernardo and Gene wound down, blood pounded in our palms and we danced off the floor. Only then did we notice bruises or welts from a misfired stick. Ironically, I never suffered an injury, although more graceful dancers did, even a few by my own hand. When the Big Group finished the dance, they broke the sticks over their knees. Ana Mari warned against that. She had to pay to replace them.

The girls had a counterpart called the ribbon dance. About twenty girls, properly spaced, stood in a large circle about thirty feet from a tall metal pole in the center. To symbolize the Basque flag, each girl held one end of a thin red, green, or white ribbon with the other end stretching to the top of the pole.

As Bernardo's accordion groaned and Gene's clarinet shrilled, half the girls stepped clockwise around the pole while the other half stepped counterclockwise. At any one time, half the girls had their arm and ribbon raised as the other half ducked under. Then the up-arms swung down and the down-arms swung up, and the raisers became the duckers. Around the metal pole they danced—arm up, arm down, arm up, arm down—half in one direction, half in the other, to the happy rhythm of accordion and clarinet. Several revolutions later, a braided pattern of red, green, and white, a replica of the Basque flag, snaked its way down the metal pole.

As Bernardo and Gene finished the song, the girls stopped their rotations and turned inward to face the pole. Their ribbons had shortened, the length consumed by the braid. The girls then retraced their steps. The clockers and counterclockers reversed their course to unbraid the ribbons as accordion and clarinet played in a flatter key to simulate an unwinding.

If one of the girls ducked under a ribbon instead of over, or moved her arm up when it should have been down, the ribbons tangled, the colored pattern became disorderly, and a rat's nest of red, green, and white knots forced Bernardo and Gene to stop their playing until a drawn-out disentanglement, not unlike a public exorcism, took place. Mikel and I figured that blame for the error was proportional to the time needed to unravel the aborted braid. The more deeply and impossibly knotted, the more a single girl ended up carrying the load for the whole messy business. That poor girl would start to cry and other girls consoled her.

The girls awed me by how intensely each concentrated and endured the public pressure to perform without mistakes lest she be skewered by her sisters. I preferred the more barbaric and less precise crashing of sticks with my Basque brothers.

The mother of all fancy feats tested lightness of foot and delicacy of touch and doled out a judgment of success or failure by the end. It was known simply as the wine dance, and both guys and girls participated. The Basques recognized that anyone who could carry out the steps deserved respect regardless of gender.

The daring dancers wore soft leather moccasins laced to the knees over thick wool socks. They set brimming glasses of wine on the cement in front of them. With hands on hips, they skipped and jumped and swirled beside and above their wineglasses. By a margin of centimeters, they nearly grazed the sides, nearly touched the edges, nearly bumped the base—but in all cases, they didn't. To do so meant utter and humiliating failure.

Dancing around the glass showed novice footwork. The great test came halfway through as dancers hopped on top of their glasses. Oh yes, *on* the glasses!

Most fat-soled mortals would think this an utter impossibility—perching toes like feathers on each side of the rim, distributing weight evenly, hopping off without spilling a drop, and then repeating the steps several times. But it happened, and a crowd served as witness each year. One wrong move—a misplaced toe, a bobble in weight, a rough moccasin, a lapse in concentration—anything really, maybe even heavy breathing—overturned and broke the glass, spilling the wine. The dancer then conceded failure—absolute and complete.

By the song's end, only the finest and most talented dancers could reach down, lift the wineglass to an appreciative audience, and yell forth a hearty *salud* as they drank it in a single gulp. The others, in sheer disgrace, stooped to collect their shards of glass, their trophies of disappointment, and mop up their spills. Many a dancer—most dancers, in fact—skulked off in shame.

I had two fat left-facing feet, which kept me out of the army and kept me from dancing on the rim of a wineglass. To stand before a crowd took courage; to dance before them even more so. But to appear before a crowd—an unruly Basque crowd—and dance around and on top of a wineglass showed grit and gallantry worthy of high praise, especially when failure brought loud public sighs and waves of inebriated hissing.

Twenty weeks later, all of my practicing brought me to the National Basque Festival in Elko during two days over the Fourth of July holiday. As early as March, the anxiety welled up in me. Toe-heel-toe-kick at the Girl Scout House offered limited embarrassment from peers who had seen and gotten used to my hopelessness. But during the festival, the eyes of the community fell on us or, more precisely, fell on *me,* I thought. Wouldn't everyone point and snicker and ask a neighbor, "Look at that boy. How could someone practice so much and still be so pathetic?"

America's birthday therefore made me ambivalent. I heralded the Fourth of July as one of my proudest days. I knew what it meant beyond fireworks. I understood it as the moment long ago when an experiment would call Dad, nearly two hundred years later, from his Basque soil, compel him to cross the Atlantic and set foot in a new land to seek a new life, new freedom, and a new chance at happiness. He would be poor in pocket, but rich in spirit. Yet here in this new nation, he would discover that limitless dividends could be derived from a man's heart and hands. His destiny would align with the destiny of his new home and he would thrive.

Mixed with this deep respect, I harbored anxiety—real, practical anxiety unknowingly heaped on me from Mom and Dad. Mom woke me early. The night before she had pressed white pants and a white short-sleeved, button-up cotton shirt with a well-starched collar. With a brown-rust-bottomed iron, she creased a red scarf from corner to corner into a perfect right triangle and draped a well-starched red sash over a hanger. She cut strands at each end to give the sash an ornamented fray and then set white tennis shoes at the foot of my bed. She had picked them up on layaway from JC Penney's or Bob's Togs. Mom and Dad didn't like debt. The shoes gleamed, laced up, ready to go, and across the toes, a pair of white socks, firm and fresh, smelling new with a bouncy, comfortable thickness.

When I went for my bath, Mom laid the ensemble across the bed and there the pieces awaited the unfortunate fulfillment of me in costume. Dad generally cared little for his own clothes, or for the clothes of me or my sister, but on this day he was uniquely attentive. He put on his glasses and reviewed the articles, making sure each was impeccable. If he encountered a spot, a wrinkle, a frayed end of the sash with one string longer than the others, he and Mom had to fix it—pull out the iron, cut the strand, re-lace the shoes, get another pair of socks.

For my part, I slowed things down. If I usually avoided a bath, I insisted on staying longer in the tub. If I resisted making my bed, now I took extra time to tuck in every sheet, straighten every blanket, and plump every pillow. Thoughts ran through my head about preferring public nudity over this costume of my forebears. I dressed with the pace of a tree lemur—white pants and white shirt, red kerchief knotted around my neck and draped down my back.

Dad wrapped the bloodred sash twice round my waist and tied it off with the frayed ends dangling by my right leg. I pulled on the socks and shoes and Dad plopped a red beret on my head, tilted ever so slightly to one side. I stood in front of the mirror, red and white and red all over, easily mistakable for a poster child of the American Red Cross.

No child so adorned could retain an ego. Apparently, however, shreds of ego remained, for I felt them stripped clean minutes later like buzzards over bones. Mom pulled bells—oh, yes, bells—from a cardboard box. They were silver jingling balls, sixteen of them, mounted in a four-by-four square on two pieces of tanned leather, thirty-two jingling bell-balls, with buckles top and bottom. Mom strapped each like shin guards on my legs. To walk was to jingle. I became tambourine boy. Any convicted burglar should have had the bells surgically attached to announce him to potential victims.

I whispered to myself, "Oh, Lord, please, please, tell me now that I am adopted. Please don't let me go outside. Break my leg, oh, Lord; a touch of bubonic plague perhaps. Find me in Your Book of Names, oh, Lord. Have me come up now. It is my time."

Mom and Dad admired their handiwork. They turned me round and round, untied and tied the cherry sash, trying to even out the frayed ends, and adjusted the jingling balls. They looked at me, looked in the mirror, and looked at each other. They both beamed as my misery brought them happiness.

On the way to the city park, Mom asked me to go inside Mayfair, a market at the center of town, and I found myself preferring a barefooted race across broken glass. But in the end she prevailed. I never won battles with Mom. I crossed the small parking lot into the store, trying desperately to step softly on toes to minimize the jingles. Inside I rummaged aisle to aisle, collecting the items on Mom's list. My red beret slid to one ear or the other, falling to the floor until I balanced it like a painter's palette on top of my head. My scarf twisted to my shoulder, and all along my jingling balls roared like sirens. Everyone in the store looked at me. Nerves and struggle brought sweat to my cheeks. I paid and got out of there. In the car, I slunk to the floor and dreamt it as a final resting place.

At Elko City Park, I met Mikel. We looked exactly alike. Most boys and men wore berets and sashes and scarves. The girls had a harder time of it. They wore red skirts, each with three black stripes near the hem, and a shirt of white lace. Nothing extraordinary, but on their heads, they wore white wraps. The wraps pulled to the back in big white balls in such a way that the final fold left two little triangles, like rabbit ears, at the top. When the headpieces were properly folded, the girls resembled walking television antennas.

Sure, my beret fell off, but I plopped it on my head and angled it in seconds. The white headdress needed straight pins and clips and safety pins to hold it in place, and if it popped off, it took half an hour to pin and clip it back in place. I told Mikel once that I saw it as origami inside a Chinese puzzle box.

The girls had to wear special moccasins similar to the ones for the wine dance. Long, thin red laces crisscrossed around their ankles and calves up to their knees and then tied off. Usually the laces loosened in an hour, fell, and bunched at the ankles. The girls then tangled in them, tripped, skinned their chins, and as they hit the ground, their white scarves popped off their heads. Then came tears. Sisyphus had an easier time with the boulder.

Over a loudspeaker, I heard Jess, Mikel's dad, who represented the voice of the Basque Festival, announcing the day's agenda and keeping thousands moving from event to event. He traded off with another guy, Bob Echeverria, at the microphone, but the baritone timbre of Jess's voice stuck most in my mind. He announced the winner of the sheepherder's bread competition. It had to be round and big as a Dutch oven—the bread, not the winner—thickly crusted, bland, yet heavy and absorbent for sopping up beans and steak juice. Anything low in carbohydrates was too dainty to sustain the well-formed bellies of thriving Basque men.

Jess managed contestants for the Irrintzi yell, though calling it a yell effectively demoted a lion to a housecat. Begoña came to the microphone. She started softly moving her tongue to outpace a hummingbird's wings. She pushed air through her teeth, raising the pitch, piercing and shrilling, until she ended after thirty seconds with a witch's screeching cackle. Begoña usually won, and rightfully so. Her Irrintzi performance, brilliantly half banshee and half human, either summoned the dead or scared the living. Basque ancestors in ghostly form stood by with hand on her shoulder and beamed proudly to hear a call they had known so well in life.

By afternoon, Jess gave first call for my favorite event—the Basque Bow Tie. A big granite ball sat atop a mound of blankets. As granite balls go, it appeared formidable and menacing, with no handles, smooth and shiny, weighing 225 pounds, like a magnificent gem set on a red velvet cushion. A crowd collected around it in a broad circle as Mikel and I watched cross-legged from the hot cement as we shared a Coke and chorizo.

A stumpy, thick man, about five feet eight, waddled to the granite ball on its blanket perch. His name—Inaki. He had flown from Spain for this event. He did not appear to be a model athlete, the epitome of health, lean and defined like a bodybuilder, but still he was a colossus of strength, thick and fleshy, arms like tree trunks and chest like a barrel, with a short, sinewy neck that melted imperceptibly into broad shoulders. His legs lacked definition—indiscernible knees, calves, and ankles—but no one doubted their strength. His head—big and round—with close-cut hair looked very much like the granite ball.

Two men wrapped a wide black sash five or six times around Inaki's waist. He raised his arms as they tied it off and cheers erupted from a large crowd.

An Irrintzi yell sliced the air to stir the blood.

Stepping back, Inaki eyed the granite ball, pacing like a wild animal. He stalked to it, putting his meaty forearms on either side of it, audibly expelling air and then inhaling heavily.

The crowd raised wine and beer and cheered.

Inaki squatted as if he was sitting in a low chair and rolled the granite ball into his lap. He bear-hugged it against his chest. The veins on his neck popped out, his face turned crimson, sweat started rolling down his cheeks.

With a bellow, he heaved the ball to his left shoulder.

The crowd went wild.

His hands balanced it there as he pushed to stand with his wide, thick legs. He leaned his head forward as though looking at his feet and rolled the ball behind his neck, across his spine, to his right shoulder. His face reddened, then purpled.

I thought the veins would burst and blood would squirt from his eyes. From the right shoulder, he rotated the ball under his chin and back to his left shoulder.

"Bat!" yelled the crowd—the number one in Basque. It might have been a game for Atlas as fellow Olympians looked on.

Anguish on his face, veins on his neck, color of his flesh—all insinuated that Inaki had tied his bow tie, that he could return the ball to the blankets and accept the adulation of the adoring crowd. But a single revolution was a paltry display of Basque manliness. Inaki continued.

He maneuvered the ball as before, from the left shoulder behind the neck to the right, under the chin and back to the left.

"Bi!" screamed the crowd, signifying the number two and working itself into a frenzy.

Someone yelled, "Hori! Hori!" a primordial grunt of Basque encouragement. Then came Irrintzi with power and clarity and length.

His muscles ached. Pipelines of blood showed blue on his arms. An artery pounded on his forehead.

After *bat* and *bi,* the crowd joyfully counted *hiru, lau, bost, sei, zazpi, zortzi, beatzi*—each in its own time, a total of nine rotations, nine bow ties. Going for a tenth, Inaki finally lunged forward and dropped his granite stone on the stacked blankets, returning his gem to the velvet. It fell with a muffled thud. He tried raising his arms, but his shoulders had become raw and pulpy.

The people whistled as he unbound the wide black sash from his waist.

He tossed the long cloth on the ball as if to say, "You are vanquished," and then he bowed to the audience. As he did, Mikel and I expected him to split in two as vertebrae crumbled.

Others tried to tie their bows, but none finished nine rotations. Inaki became king for a day.

I sat mesmerized on the hot sidewalk until Jess announced that the Young Group—my group—would next dance the *jota* and the *porrusalda.*

My anxiety went into overdrive. I gathered with the other minion boys, all of whom had scuffed pants and shirts and sweaty berets. The girls had given up tying and retying the head scarves and had resorted to an arsenal of straight pins, bobby pins, safety pins, and every other type of metal clip to hold them in place. They had advanced from antennas to lightning rods. Some of the laces had fallen to ankles so often that many mothers in frustration had duct-taped the laces above the knees under the skirt.

Ana Mari stood at the head of our line. Alternating boy-girl-boy-girl, we joined hands and skipped after her as Bernardo and Gene played from a platform over Jess's microphone. The bells on our shins jingled. A beret fell off from one of us. Laces came down. We looked like a cavorting chain gang of little people. We formed two lines behind our patron saint, Ana Mari, as the crowd looked on and clapped and cheered our arrival on the hot cement. The sun beat down and squinted our eyes. The music touched our ears, and our feet moved—toe-heel-toe-kick, and toe-heel-toe-kick, and now twirl, and side-to-side, and side-to-side, and twirl again, and left-and-right and right-and-left and no shuffle, shuffle and point the toes, and so on. I worked no better in public than in practice. Oh, futility, thy name is *jota*.

A local photographer snapped my photograph, immortalizing my glorious missteps and displaying them as a tourist attraction at the Elko County Convention Center. The universe had a well-placed sense of humor. God had an ironical side.

Then it ended for another year. Agustín won the wood-chopping competition, axing his way through five logs, as he would year after year before retiring his axe and returning to Spain.

Men carried hundred-pound weights in each hand for a distance of fifty yards, circled a barrel, and returned. Whoever carried them farthest won a hundred dollars.

Stephanie and Ricardo danced as a pair in the *jota* dance-off and took first place, as they did (and still do) every year. Their textbook precision of toes-and-heels and side-to-sides and graceful spins convinced me that running in their blood was a genetic predisposition for the Basque craft and a gift of dexterity and art uncommonly found in most humans.

A reporter from *Nevada Magazine* approached me and Mikel and asked us to find a few of our friends, clothed as we were in misery, and pose for a picture. We pulled in Greg and Tim and Joe. The five of us looked young, pudgy-faced, and buck-toothed. Our berets and scarves glowed like maraschino cherries against the vibrant snow white of our shirts. We might have been cartoon characters if we hadn't looked so authentic.

In its next edition, *Nevada Magazine* ran the photograph on a deep blue cover under the heading BASQUE FESTIVALS, OLD-COUNTRY GOOD TIMES IN ELKO, ELY AND RENO and pulled the photo from its files periodically to rerun it long after we had grown up and left Elko for other dances in life.

By late afternoon, many left for home in search of siestas. In the evening, they made their way to the Elko County Fairgrounds for fireworks. Dad had barbecued all day, standing in the sun and serving up a thousand steaks. Mom had fought to keep my white pants white and Jonna's head scarf pinned and her shoes laced. Both Mom and Dad looked tired. Grayness ringed their eyes.

How did I endure these days? Why did Mom and Dad force me to endure them? Youth had a way of clouding the obvious.

Mom and Dad wanted to ground us to deep bedrock of good people and unique events. They wanted to plant our feet solidly in common, familiar soil and make us part of an extended family. Without this communal link, they regarded us as rootless, shallow in our underpinnings, and susceptible to bending and breaking from the mildest winds. They insisted by their raising that we would not be free of moorings or anchorless. We would have a touchstone, many touchstones. If ever in our future we felt adrift, we would have those moments and memories of good people, sensible people whom we could call upon in the darkest hours for strength and guidance, reassurance and spirit. They would steel our minds and restore joy to our hearts. They became rocks—Gibraltars, one and all.

With beret, scarf, sash, and bells, with skirt, headdress, leg laces, and moccasins, with wine and wood, granite balls and piercing screams, ribbons and sticks, *jotas* and *porrusaldas*—through them all—year after year, Mom and Dad forged links in a long chain that stretched from Elko to Spain and thence into antiquity.

Boundless and unending, the links reached to aunts and uncles and cousins, Grandma and Grandpa, anguished faces bombed in Guernica, oak trees and convents, fishermen and farmers, battles won and lost, whale and cod, endurance and survival.

The chain grew long and strong—no iron compared. Each link became wider by its length.

As time inched forward, a new duty arose in me to carry and not shun the links to those who came before me. I walked in the footsteps of my fathers' past. In carrying this chain of my forebears, I found nothing but the lightness of honor.

## 13

Eight days of our Spanish trip had made Dad tired. He slept well each night, took his heart pills, and napped each afternoon, but the riding, walking, and visiting wore down his seventy-eight-year-old body.

As we drove from Palencia, he leaned his head against the window while I bore on to Mondragón, one of our final stops.

Within twenty minutes, Dad's breathing turned to snores as we passed a few houses, a bar, and a couple of shops. A sign said LEAVING TORQUEMADA. I knew the name.

After the ascension of Queen Isabella in the fifteenth century, Torquemada, her private confessor, became the Grand Inquisitor of Spain. Under his ministrations, the Inquisition grew from a single tribunal in Seville to a network of Holy Offices, including at the Cathedral of Palencia, to ferret out Jews, Muslims, and Marranos, Christian converts who secretly practiced Judaism or Islam. He pursued orthodoxy of faith while zealots in church and government crafted a campaign of *sangre limpia*—clean blood—a crusade that transformed Torquemada's ambitions into practical application.

To purify Spain, he turned to the Spanish people, who obeyed lest he point a bony finger in their direction and inflict punishment on them. He issued guidelines instructing people to observe their neighbors and turn them in if they wore fancy clothes, cleaned their homes on Friday, lit candles at night, ate unleavened bread, began meals with celery and lettuce during Holy Week, or prayed facing a wall while bowing back and forth.

During his fifteen-year reign, more than two thousand souls burned, but the manner of death, the intensity of pain, and the duration depended on the willingness of alleged offenders to confess their sins, denounce their gods, and accept Christ into their hearts. Torquemada sought to nurture and protect Spain's Catholic ascendancy.

After the Moors were conquered in 1491, and Granada surrendered a year later, the Jews felt pressure from the *sangre limpia* campaign. Two influential Jews went to Isabella and offered thirty thousand ducats to allow their kind to stay in the country. When Torquemada heard of this, he told Isabella that "Judas sold his Master for thirty ducats. You would sell Him for thirty thousand. Take Him and sell Him, but do not let it be said that I have had any share in this transaction."

Within a year, his life's work culminated in the Edict of Expulsion, which commanded Jews to leave Spain and never return. Torquemada then retired to the monastery of Saint Thomas in Avila, where he died six years later.

Approaching Burgos as Dad snored deeply, I considered Torquemada's villainy no great surprise since evil men littered the pages of history and often enlisted common citizens to aid their campaigns. I found no surprise either in a queen who purported to be enlightened but delegated ruthless authority to advance malevolent ends. Many royalists in history had welded disparate parts of empire by focusing on a common enemy.

But Torquemada's grandmother surprised me. She had been Jewish most of her life and converted to Christianity before her death. By his own definition, his grandmother lacked orthodoxy of faith and Torquemada lacked *sangre limpia,* but he hid his roots. To live denied his past, to carry out his deeds vilified his blood. I imagined that he loathed himself and it poisoned his spirit, making each day a chore, each minute a labor.

Anyone who concealed such a secret could not show a warm heart. Inner turmoil led to external destruction and made redemption unattainable so long as truth to one's past remained elusive. A personal transgression pained the heart. Redemption healed it by asking forgiveness, extending a hand, receiving acceptance, and sealing the beauty in a warm hug.

Yet how, I wondered, did victims of national sin find solace and comfort? How did a whole nation that built an apparatus of death, denied justice, and burned books only to burn humans in the end, wash stains from its national conscience? And if that was left undone, could a people ever find relief?

In Burgos, I pulled the Subaru into a service station to buy gas and pick up snacks to stave off Dad's diabetic shakes.

"Did you have a good sleep?"

"I good all day now," he said.

"I'm curious, Dad."

"Oh shit!"

"What do you mean?"

"Every time you curious, my head hurt."

I ignored him and asked my question. "Do you think that the Basques got over what Franco did to them?"

"What you mean?"

"I mean bombing Gernika, closing schools, levying taxes, keeping you from speaking the language, locking people up, and killing them for thirty years."

"Dat long time ago."

"I know, but what do you think?"

"I don' think 'bout dat."

"Never?"

"I did once when I left Spain. I don' want to go at first."

"Why not?"

"I worry 'bout Momma and Daddy. If I leave, what happen to dem. Franco, he round up people, put dem in prison. Dey disappear and den good-bye, Charlie, never see dem again."

"You worried that might happen to them?"

"Dat's right."

"How'd you get over that?"

"I didn'. I worry 'til dey die. We call dem every Christmas, your mama and me. I hear deir voices and dey okay. Den next day, I worry 'bout dem again. Makes my belly hurt."

"But when they died your belly stopped hurting?"

"Dat's right. Dey go to heaven so dey okay."

"You said you didn't want to go at first. Who made you go?"

"Daddy, he say he don' want me here and I need to go to Tío Vicente. Dat's his brother."

"Has that ever bothered you?"

"What?"

"That Grandpa sent you away?"

"You know—see if you understand me—when I herdin' sheep I think he send me away 'cause I one more mouth, and dere's no food. I reason—no, no—how you say dat word?"

"Resented?"

"Yes. I resented Daddy." Then counting on his fingers, "He keep 'nita, Juanita, Isabella, Fakunda, Joakin, Pilar, and Juan, but he let me go. I resent dat. Den when I see Tío Vicente, his brother, I think he just the same."

"You resented him too."

"Dat's right."

"But you don't anymore."

"No. Daddy, he do de right thing. He know dere's no chance for one life in Spain, but dere's one chance in United States. He been to America. He knew. I figure dat out when I buy de Star Hotel."

"And then you didn't resent Grandpa anymore?"

"Dat's right."

"Or Tío Vicente?"

"Yes. Tío Vicente, he one strong man, strongest I ever seen. He work hard every day, all crippled up. Your uncle John, you know he walk with one walker?"

"Yes."

"Well, Tío Vicente, he jus' the same, but he don' have no walker. He had one cane, he bent over and twisted up, and he work 'til he ninety years old. He get up one night to go de bathroom and he fall down and he hit his head on de bathtub and good-bye, Charlie. He didn' wake up. He de man I most ever respected. You named for him."

"Mom told me that you and she had decided to name me Martin for her father, but then after I was born, you named me Vicente after your uncle and signed the birth certificate while she slept. She wasn't happy. She still tells that story and she's still mad at you."

"I don' think so. It don' matter."

"I still think it's sad, Dad."

"What sad?"

"That any mother or father sends his child away. How do you think Grandpa felt about that?"

"I 'member. He and Momma, dey pretty sad. Daddy, he know what he doing. But I think if Momma, she had one gun, she would've shot Franco dead. She mad as hell."

While I held no recollection of Grandpa, I had met my grandmother twice, first when I was two years old. After three of my dirty diapers, she filled a basin with ice water and, much to the anger of my own mother, sat me waist deep in it. By the end of the trip, I returned to the United States potty trained.

When the family visited Spain eight years later, I saw a brawny, powerful woman of eighty-two years who woke each morning to collect wood, start her potbelly stove, boil coffee, and cook. Her white hair, pulled back with clips and pins, bespoke a profound wisdom. She had sat in the kitchen with husband and children during cold nights with little food, and her voice did not break the air next to her husband, Mariano, who spoke for the household, advised the children, and made the decisions. She absorbed everything. But after all those years of listening, a feeling came from her that said she had something important to share. Her hands, chafed and rough from toiling in fields, scratched my skin as she rubbed my cheeks.

I saw a potent image in that kitchen. There sat my grandmother, a rugged woman, independent and sure, with strength and determination, who cared for eight children, keeping them safe through civil war and decades of occupation. Years later, I imagined her foraging scraps of bread, mending unmendable clothes, making fire with wet wood, and playing the fool to fool the guards. I couldn't imagine her anguish at sending a child away, even to America. I thought her an unlikely warrior, who wore no medals and showed no pride but deserved both. I wondered who noted her achievements or those of all mothers the world over.

"Did Grandma ever get over her anger?" I asked Dad.

"I don' know—prob'ly. See if you understand me. Momma and Daddy, dey get to one point when dey don' live no more for demselves. Dey jus' survive. Dey try to do good for deir chil'ren. Dey don' got noding for demselves, so dey try to make sure deir chil'ren got someding. If dey see someding good for me and 'nita and Juanita and Pilar and de oders, den dey don' get anger no more."

"So they can forgive if their children do well."

"Dat's right."

"And if their children don't do well?"

"Den I don' know."

"After I sell de Star and I come back here, Momma and Daddy, dey see me okay and dey okay after dat."

"What about moms and dads who lost children, or children who lost moms and dads, or people taken to prison who didn't come back? How about them?"

"I don' know."

"You know what I think, Dad?"

"What's dat?"

"I think the only way forgiveness comes is if people who survived remember those who died. They have to tell the stories so we get to hear about their lives, and the government has to tell the truth about what happened and the pain it caused. Then the ones who lived can move on, and who knows, maybe those who died can too. You think Spain will ever do that for all the years Franco ruled?"

"Don' know. Maybe don' matter."

"Why not?"

"I not dink dis 'fore we come here. But I dink before someding like dat happen, dere no more Basco 'round. Dey all dis'pear," he said, turning to the window. Continuing, he said almost as an afterthought, "But Momma, if she 'round, she like someding like dat."

## 14

Had dressing and dancing in red sash, scarf, and beret been my only torment, I might have swallowed the ancestral obligation without a word. But moving by my sixth birthday from the Blue Jay Bar to a small sheep farm on the outskirts of town gave me responsibilities that tested my loyalty as a good son.

The window of my room looked over three acres of short bluegrass that edged up to mountains of burnt gray sagebrush. A single elm grew in the far corner of our field. It had been struck by lightning three or four times, as though nature like an artist had rubbed her thumb to wipe it from the scene, but the elm resisted and stood upright and strong.

I peered through that window as I got up each morning and before I went to bed at night, and I saw the same thing—sheep pulling up grass, sheep with legs folded under, sheep sipping from a trough, sheep standing and staring at nothing—all the time, every hour of every day—sheep, sheep, sheep.

Our field wasn't fenced on two sides, but steep hills served as natural barriers against any one sheep leading the rest off a cliff. Sheep were naive, innocent creatures with a musketeer complex—where one went, so they all went. They shared a kind of collective intelligence, or rather a collective stupidity.

A sheep once poked its head through a wire fence reaching for a weed ten feet away. When it fell nine feet short, it pulled back to find the wire biting into its wool. It nearly strangled until I freed it. I told Dad about it and he said, "Dat's normal."

For years, we planted a garden in our front yard, a plot of land much smaller than our acreage in the back, but still as fertile. I watched Dad raise a hoe to strike the earth and bring up clods, a poor man's tilling. He worked the weekend to turn twenty-eight rows of crusted dirt for seeding corn, beans, potatoes, carrots, squash, and the occasional pumpkin. Dusk came and his palms blistered and bled as the last row of moist soil took form and crumbled inch by inch between his boots.

He exerted as much effort during the harvest, pulling up cornstalks and deeply rooted potato plants or carting off the spiny pumpkin leaves and prickly bean vines.

When annual tilling and harvesting became too much for him, he planted alfalfa to supplement the sheep's food supply instead of ours. Ordinarily, the sheep ate crabgrass, bluegrass, or parts of Russian thistle, and happily munched and shit without a care. But when the alfalfa grew thick and full, and Dad let them loose to graze, they appeared downright giddy and gleeful to frolic in the stuff, like a kid swimming in a vat of chocolate or rolling in jelly beans.

Within twenty minutes, one ewe ate so much that her belly blew up like a balloon and Dad had to puncture her side with a pocketknife to release the air. Had he not acted quickly, the gluttonous beast would have popped, toppled to her side, and died. Sheep survived in spite of themselves.

"You watch dem. Ten minutes, no more. If dey blowed up, den you poke dem with one knife, and den take dem back dere," Dad told me.

"What if they don't want to go?"

"Dey won't go, I promise dat. You make dem go."

Avoiding gastronomical explosions did not appeal to me, and I worried about having to knife the ewes in the side or, worse, watch them topple and die, so I hedged and cut their eating to seven minutes, and herded them to the barn three minutes shy of their promised smorgasbord.

Between mouthfuls, sheep randomly took up what Dad called "singin'." A ewe would bleat, and for no reason at all another would pick up the call. Another would follow and then another, and soon the woolly lot of them would join a chorus—high-pitched screams from the lambs and dry-throated baritones from the long-toothed mothers. All one hundred of them would take turns breaking the quiet of the field, and then just as suddenly resume their munching. Mysterious imbeciles, that's what I called them.

Sheep became a central tool of my education, often without me realizing it. In the summer after my sixth-grade year, I heard Mom say, "Joe, talk to him."

"What I say to him?" responded Dad.

From the hallway, I listened to their cryptic exchange. Had I asked them, both would have denied that they were talking about me, so I waited for one of them to act. It was Dad.

"Come to barn with me," Dad said. His tone seemed odd. Usually, I could tell why he needed me from something in his demeanor, volume, or hand movements, but not today.

"For what?"

"You jus' come." And so I followed, a few feet behind, as a matter of custom.

A few days before, Dad had rented a buck from Paris Ranch. It roamed our small acreage, marking its territory like a dog, and stamping its broad black hooves at me, Dad, the dog, or anyone who dared to trespass into its domain. It stood tall and wide like a square, sturdy brick covered in wool, and when it moved, it did not walk, it pranced with a proud, egotistical swagger. It had mean, slanted eyes, a look of defiance and domination. If feeling threatened, the buck could charge and catapult its 250-pound body headfirst like a torpedo into an unsuspecting target. Though coming up on the seventh grade, I feared the animal, and knowing that Dad had forbidden me to enter the acreage alone, I knew that my fear was entirely justified.

At the barn, we stood side by side near the trough and hung our arms over the wire fence. The whole scene froze like a single frame from a picture show—the trough below showed no waves, the water bugs slept in the corners and didn't skim the surface, and the emerald moss, usually swaying beneath, seemed to hold a wispy pose to one side; the air, hot and dry, gave no hint of breeze and carried no scent of sweet sage, leaving only a stale blandness, a taste of gray under an otherwise searing sun; the ewes appeared stuck in place, as though their hooves had taken root, and betraying only the slightest nods, their hanging heads pulled up shoots of summer grass with mouths chewing in slow motion.

"What are we doing here?" I asked.

"Shhh. You quiet," whispered Dad. He took off his cap and held it to his side.

We stood and stared and said nothing, becoming a part of the frozen picture, subject to the same unnatural rules that governed the day. The stillness had no reprieve.

I fidgeted.

"Shhh," Dad spit out, not even turning his head to look at me.

"What are we doing here?" I whispered again.

"Be quiet. You watch."

The buck came slowly across the field, a solitary figure of power like a living soul among the dead, seeing everything yet remaining unseen. It touched a ewe with its furry black nose, sniffed, and stamped a foot, and then went to another ewe, where it sniffed again, deep and loud, breaking the silence of the day.

"What's it doing?"

"Shhh."

Circling behind the ewe, the buck suddenly reared on its hind legs and crashed its muscular front quarters heavily onto the ewe's back. She screamed. Her planted hooves remained cemented in place and her thin legs nearly buckled at the knees. The buck rocked back and forth as the ewe groaned. For fifteen seconds, I watched with embarrassment as Dad turned me into a barnyard voyeur to satisfy his fatherly version of birds-and-bees. Fully spent, the buck dismounted.

Dad looked down at me and questioned, rhetorically, "Understand?" and then not waiting for any kind of reply, he put on his cap and walked back to the house. I followed at a short distance, watching the buck as before, but for now it seemed less a threat, tired and ready for sleep.

Inside, I went to my room and buried my humiliated face in a pillow.

"Did you talk to him?" I heard Mom ask from the kitchen.

"I talk to him," Dad replied.

She was pleased.

Opposite my bedroom wall outside, Dad set up a short, sturdy table, about a foot from the ground, with steel pipes for legs and a plywood top. Blood had seeped into the swirling patterns of the knotted wood. It made an attractive pattern as long as you ignored the medium.

About ten feet above the macabre table, an iron railing much like a gymnast's high bar had been outfitted with pulleys, ropes, and four or five hooks, reminiscent of Torquemada's Spanish Inquisition.

"I need your help," Dad whispered close to my ear.

"Right now?"

"Yes."

I could tell from the soft tone and the closeness to my ear that he didn't plan to build a fence, mend a barn, or move sprinklers. Nor, thankfully, did he plan a voyeur's reenactment of bucks and ewes. We had death to do. Under these conditions, I always felt reluctant.

Through the back door of our house, I moved to the other side of my bedroom window, through the looking glass, and stood by the bloodstained table.

From his pocket, he pulled out a knife with a pointed four-inch blade and an ivory grip that gleamed in the cold October sun. He held it in his right hand as he walked out to the silent ewes tearing up grass and fattening their bellies.

Coming up from behind, he grabbed the leg of one and she screamed with fright, as anyone might if snatched in surprise from a dinner plate. The other ewes and lambs began their chorus—loud, fast, staccato—bleats of warning and caution, voices of danger and alertness.

He dragged the ewe until she fell on her haunches and her front legs splayed ahead, and then he pulled her up to her hindquarters, belly displayed, and tightened his legs and feet, like a vise, on either side of her.

With one hand, he cradled her black nose, touching the thin skin underneath to expose the throat, and then plunged the gleaming blade of the ivory knife into her neck. He winced at the moment of the prick.

Naturally she fought and groaned as he sliced a half circle through the thick wool. The red gushed. He bent the head back and the spine cracked as the ewe wriggled and jerked. His legs on either side held firm.

As life left her, she exerted enormous energy, kicks and spasms from four legs and hooves and a worthless dangling head. The other sheep—all of them—bleated with full-throated voices, loud and constant, over and over. These mammalian hymns were a funeral dirge.

I had heard often that it was darkest before the dawn. But here, as a child, I wondered in reverse if the greatest light came at the moment of eternal darkness. I tried to catch the life force from a trillion cells drawing together into a ball and escaping the dying body. I looked for the conversion, the soul leaving the vacant shell and ascending. I missed it.

Dad withdrew the knife from the neck as the jerking ended and limbs went limp. He wiped the blade twice on his pants. With one hand, he dragged the carcass from the field to the butcher's block, where I stood as the head scraped across the ground streaking blood in the grass. The long black ears flopped and an image of a stillborn lamb leapt into my mind. He heaved the dead weight onto the table and went to work unsheathing the meat.

Sweat dripped from his nose and chin and he breathed deeply and muscles on his arms tightened and strained. Wrangling life from a creature exacted as much energy from the wrangler as from the wrangled. Killing took something out of a man.

I never warmed to the ending of life and the beginning of the hereafter. The severed throat and the smell of blood turned my stomach, though I helped Dad without a peep of protest. I sensed life all around—sister sheep howled, the elm in the corner swayed, flies buzzed, grass moved, magpies swooped. Ordinarily I missed these things, but engulfed by death, life showed through.

Singular moments had a way of gaining weight and becoming heavy. Customarily, we thought every second had equal say in a minute, and every minute spoke with equal force in an hour. But each second carried its own weight, sometimes the weight of years or a lifetime—Gernika, Hiroshima, Kennedy's death, Chernobyl, 9/11, the Crucifixion. A second felt so heavy sometimes that it sliced time in two, creating a before and an after and leaving us forever changed.

Poking the neck, gushing the blood, and cracking the vertebrae defined a heavy second for me.

I separated my responsibilities from Dad's to lighten this load. I told myself that I aided in the butchering and not in the slaughter, serving as accomplice, to be sure, but not instigator. I held a leg as he broke the ankles, severed the hooves, and hooked the Achilles' tendons to ready the hang. I pulled the rope to hoist the carcass as he stripped away the last vestiges of wool. I shooed the flies from his forehead and toweled blood from his forearms as he finished the gut. I was not executioner, though I moved the basket to catch the head.

Fine lines, perhaps, but the distinction was akin to being the midwife and not the mother, the mortician and not the axe wielder. Only one in each pairing endured the true weight of the ordeal.

I spread the sheepskin like a rug in a wheelbarrow and pushed it beneath the hung ewe so the guts could be spilled out. The smell made my eyes water. A green mush of undigested grass surrounded the organs like insulation. Dad cut out stomach and intestine, liver and kidneys. He hosed out the inside from top to bottom.

I wheeled the jumbled guts to his blue pickup, folded the edges of sheepskin over the innards, and lifted the ghoulish package to the tailgate. I gagged as I slid the whole messy business into the truck bed so Dad could deliver it to the city dump. As much as I tried, I could not keep the smell from covering me. It stayed for a week.

I brought Dad a pot of water from the kitchen so he could save the fresh liver and kidneys. Within six hours of the butchering, he would cook them with onions and garlic and sit down with a loaf of French bread and feast with joy.

He picked up the sheep's head by one of its black floppy ears and put it in a plastic bag to give later to Chapo, of *mus*-playing fame, who would store it up until he had four heads to cook together.

Chapo would strip the black-faced skin and bake the heads upright on a cookie sheet in the oven. Through the window on the stove, the four faces looked out, their fatty white flesh being tanned by the red element.

Chapo would relish his meal and start the same way. He would pluck a moist eyeball from a socket and bite into it. The warm juices, still preserved inside, would pop and run down his chin. Even when I expected it, his etiquette tormented me while he reveled in the teasing and the taste and laughed heartily from his round belly.

I never ate Chapo's delights. But Dad's likes shaped my own from those earliest days sitting on his lap swigging beer or wine at the Blue Jay Bar. After he cooked the liver and kidneys, an odor of iron wafted through the house and floated there for a week, filling our nostrils at bedtime and welcoming us in the morning. Next to him at our kitchen counter, I choked down a chunk of liver with an oversized wad of bread as he ravenously stuffed piece after piece into his mouth and soaked up the grease to top off the last morsel. The taste sickened me, but I ate it to satisfy him.

He seemed unfazed by slaughtering or butchering. Each winter our freezer filled with chops and ribs and roasts and legs of lamb. We didn't want for anything. He seemed the connoisseur of slaughter.

Still, I wondered if it bothered him, even a little bit. I saw him wince when he poked the neck, and then curl his tongue between his teeth and lips when he pulled back the head to widen the cut, gush the blood, and snap the backbone. The wince might have been more than a facial tic. Perhaps he recognized that taking life, any life, required a greater purpose—to feed a family, safeguard a home, defend a nation.

"Can I cut the sheep's neck?" I asked him once. I did not want to, but I wanted to for him, figuring that to do as he did endeared me to him, made him love me by doing what he loved.

"I got to do it," he replied, and he didn't give up the knife.

"I can do it, Dad." I had turned eight by then and felt older, stronger, and wiser. I saw it as a rite of passage.

"No. Some oder time."

Months passed or a year, and I asked him again, "Can I cut the sheep's neck?"

"No. I got to do it." He said the same way. I resented the decision.

"Why won't you let me?"

"I do it," he said, "so you don' have to."

## 15

Nearly two hundred miles placed me and Dad beyond Palencia, Torquemada, and Burgos and a stone's throw from Mondragón, where Tía Pilar, Tío Pedro, and Cousin Amaia lived. The road wound like a serpent through the Pyrenees foothills, passing red clay cottages and taverns dating back five centuries. The path was narrow and populated with sheep or goats herded by wrinkled shepherds. Children bounded over small hills to retrieve rocks and sticks, the local equivalent of baseballs and bats, and some distance away, a frumpy Basque man in a black beret, perhaps a caretaker, with hoe in hand, pulled up clods of earth.

"Dis look de same," Dad said.

"What looks the same?"

"Everyding. I know dis."

The whole picture felt common and comfortable, like worn shoe leather. Had Dad and I traveled these parts one or two centuries earlier, we would have seen the same red clay homes, the same sheep and goats, the same children chasing rocks and sticks, and the same old men tearing up dirt to plant the same seeds.

Change did not come easily here. Present and future were anchored in the past. What we saw and felt, we could see and feel twenty or fifty years from now if we returned. I found comfort in that notion.

In the United States, Dad and I had often heard that resisting change was tantamount to fearing progress. As we waited for sheep and goats to cross, I watched a barefooted man sow his garden. He made a shallow trench, laid seed, and added water. In time, he would harvest grapes and vegetables to make wine and feed his family. No—this man was not afraid, nor were other men who chose his life. I wondered in fact who showed more fear: this simple man standing in the dirt growing life or the sophisticated man crouching behind mountains of complexity, legality, and technology in defense of progress.

Past the sheep and goats, we came to a highway still under construction. Despite two lanes in both directions and a modern line of fluorescent panels and street lamps, our car traveled alone for miles, making me think that we had turned wrong and would soon hit a gap in the road and plunge a hundred feet to our doom.

"One beautiful road," Dad said admiringly.

"If you came to Spain for the road," I said. "I wonder if the towns under the road will survive." The highway had been elevated on concrete columns above a sprinkling of homes a hundred feet below. In a few cases, the highway did not offer an exit to reach these communities, so I wondered if they would thrive in isolation as they had for countless generations, or if they would suffer for lack of commerce.

"Dey be fine," Dad said. "Dey been here a thousand years."

"I hope so."

Just then, I sensed a gloominess in the air, something that had been there all along during our eight days in Spain, but only now did I piece together small details to arrive at this perception. Having visited Spain in the past, I knew that the country had enjoyed cheerier days, but clearly world events had taken their toll. The economic downturn had raised unemployment, dropped stock values, collapsed the housing industry, and left consumers reeling from debt. A sense of panic filled the air, and no one seemed to know how or why the crisis had started or how to fix it. The United States had responded reflexively, in Keynesian style, spending literally trillions of dollars to unfreeze credit and lubricate world markets.

When Dad and I came off the new highway into Mondragón's town square, it was deserted. The only roaming soul was a wrinkled woman with a downcast head, a dark jacket, and a slow, even pace. She walked as if she was pulling one foot at a time from thick mud. We drove alongside her as Dad yelled a question from the window, but she didn't raise her head, miss a step, or acknowledge our presence. She retreated into deep thought, a hostage of her own depressed world.

We parked the car near a grove of leafless, knobby trees, the same kind we had found in Lekeitio, with the same efficient, non-aesthetical close trim, and I called Cousin Amaia to come find us.

While waiting, Dad and I counted three stragglers with the same dour expressions as the old woman. They appeared from around corners and quickly disappeared inside one of the shuttered buildings.

"How dis town work?"

"What do you mean?"

"No people, no cars, no business. How dis town not just die?"

It reminded me of the old men and women of Gernika, tired and worn, asleep on park benches, entering their twilight years.

"Well, Dad, it's Sunday," I said. "Some towns don't let businesses open on Sunday. The workers stay home."

"You think so?"

"Not sure, but I know Mondragón does more business than this."

The sleepy image belied Mondragón's true economic strength as a federation of worker cooperatives. As a businessman, I had partnered with several employee-owned companies in the technology sector around Washington, DC. Each had prospered, but none to the degree seen in Mondragón. In the mid-fifties, nearly ten years after Dad had come to the United States, a young priest had first broached the idea of joining people into a sovereignty of labor placing human needs at the center and business interests on the periphery. Built around finance, industry, retail, and education, the cooperatives in time expanded to seventeen countries, produced billions in revenue, and yielded some of the highest profits of any corporation in Spain. Now, half a century later, the cooperatives had helped make northern Spain, and the Basque Country particularly, one of the strongest industrial centers throughout the nation, if not all of Europe.

Cousin Amaia took us to Tía Pilar's home, where the drab did not follow us inside. As we took a slow elevator to the fourth floor, I asked her, "Why does Mondragón seem so sad?"

"Sunday," she said. "Nothing open."

"Dat's what I tell him," said Dad. I growled at him.

Tía Pilar gave off her own light that lent brightness and joy to everyone around her. She clasped her hands under an elegant smile that said, "Oh, thank all in heaven, you are most welcome here."

Her blond hair, parted and lying to one side, was as radiant as a fashion magazine, hardly befitting a woman of seventy-four years, but like the rest of her, it shined like silk. She kissed me and Dad several times and then ordered Tío Pedro to relieve us of our suitcases immediately. Quiet and compliant, he said only, "Yes, dear."

Had her slender frame allowed, she might have gladly lifted and carried us like kings to our room. More aptly, had Tío Pedro, now in his eighties, been younger and stronger, she might have ordered him to do it.

I loved everything about Tía Pilar, not only because she plied us with food and drink, tended to our whims, and anticipated our every need even before we knew we had one. I loved her because of how rarely I encountered a selfless, happy warrior with a good soul whose chief ambition was to make others feel safe and comfortable, not just in her home but in life.

Tía Pilar once had a calling to be a nun. It pulled at her hard. Had she accepted the calling, she said, her nothingness would have been given over for His greater glory, a life of good deeds, prayer, and hard work.

This word *calling* I understood well whenever I heard it. Out of college, I had received several offers on Wall Street from investment bankers or brokerage houses, each promising wonderful salaries for the time, complete with bonuses and lucrative perks. I decided instead to oversee public housing complexes and work with the poor in Colorado, Wyoming, Utah, North Dakota, South Dakota, and Montana. My friends thought me crazy and tried to dissuade me, telling me that I would regret the decision. But I had reasoned that nothing so strong could be a mistake, so I started the work. My pockets remained empty, but my spirit was full. From then on, I gained moments of joy from the experience, as Tía Pilar, I now imagined, found similar happiness.

She said she knew her calling to be true and right. Anything so powerful that inspired good works, she said, could have only come from God, and not from any force of or under the earth. She could not ignore it.

"But you're not a nun," I said. "You must have ignored it."

"No, no." She wagged her finger. "If you can't obey His rules with your whole heart, then you can't accept the calling. It is a choice."

"So your heart wasn't in it?" I asked.

"Not all the way." She looked at Tío Pedro and touched his face.

"But that doesn't mean you don't honor the calling in your own way, even if you fall short every day," she said.

Tía Pilar had a rare humility. She had used the word *nothingness* to describe herself, suggesting a lack of confidence, but no one who touched her or anyone whom she touched could walk away confused. She had a charisma born of this nothingness. She spent little time on self. She gave her energy away, funneled it into hard work and good deeds. From nothingness came selflessness, which attracted people who sought this great lightness of being.

After we were settled, Tía Pilar pulled us to dinner. She had prepared delicacies—*lebatza* fried in egg, broiled cow's tongue, lentil soup, bread, and a sugar-coated, cream-filled pastry for dessert. The meal lasted two hours. I vowed to avoid food for a week—my kingdom for a light salad.

"You are getting fat," she said, rubbing Dad's belly all over like Buddha as she collected plates.

"Too much food," Dad replied.

"You have too much, and others not enough," she retorted.

"Oh, Ama, don't start," said Cousin Amaia, dropping her head into her hands.

Conversation melted into a hodgepodge of Basque, Spanish, and English that offered something for everyone at the table—me and Dad, Pilar and Pedro, Amaia and Juan Madi, her husband. For whatever I couldn't understand, I continually prodded Dad and Amaia for translations.

"Don't start what?"

Tía Pilar turned to me and asked, "What do you think about the economy?"

"I think it's a mess," I said.

"And who made the mess?"

"I think there's blame to go around."

"I tell you where there's blame—greed. Everyone wants money. They want this or that, new houses and new cars. They want it all and don't want to pay for it. You think I'm right?"

"I think that's part of it," I said.

"Of course it is." She cut into the dessert, piled on whipped cream, and passed plates around. "People don't wait to get things. They want them now. Countries do the same. Some countries have lots and others have nothing."

Turning to Dad, I said, "You didn't tell me that your sister was a spitfire."

"Lots of talk," Dad said.

Tía Pilar hopped up from the table as though she sat on a spring and scampered down the hallway. Returning quickly, she set on the table a photograph framed in cardboard.

"This boy," she said, "is in San Salvador—pobre. He doesn't have anything. Every month I give him money for food and books."

"Waste of money," Dad snorted.

"Por que?"

"Because dat boy, he never see your money. Government take it," Dad replied.

"You sound like a revolutionary," I told her. "Libertad, Igualdad, Fraternidad!" I repeated the old rallying cry of the French.

"Yes! If a revolutionary thinks children should have plenty to eat, and a roof over their head, and a school to go to, then I am a revolutionary. Everyone talks about ending poverty, but no one does it. More people in poverty now than ever. Lots of promises."

Then she raised her arm to mimic the Statue of Liberty, widened her eyes, and stared ahead.

Cousin Amaia again dropped her head into her hands and Juan Madi giggled. Tío Pedro continued eating dessert without a peep.

Sitting back down, she said, "But I am old now and these are young ideas."

"Good ideas are never young or old. They are ageless," I said. She smiled at me, put her palms on my cheeks, and squeezed my lips with a kind of rough affection.

"If you work," Dad said, "den you eat. If you can't work, den a little help okay. But some people, dey jus' bums. Dey don' work and don' want to work and dey expect someone else to pay for dem."

"To work, you need jobs," countered Tía Pilar.

"Dere's work. Dere's work everywhere. Lots of people, dey don' want to open deir eyes and see de work. Dey go to college and want one big job. But den who mops de floor? Who trim de trees? Who clean de toilets? Dere's work all over de place. People don' want to do it."

"The government needs to make good jobs for people," said Tía Pilar.

"Government don' make noding," said Dad. "One person with one idea, he make de jobs. If he work hard and he make money, den he keep what he make."

"Oh, Jose, Jose," said Tía Pilar, shaking her head. "The money is controlled by corporations. No people can have good ideas. The corporations steal them. I tell you what. The government should break them up and give the money to people who need food and a bed."

She pointed to the picture of the small boy from San Salvador.

"Corporations, dey make a lot," said Dad, nearly conceding the point. "But you open de doors and government, it never go out. Dey mess everyding up, take all de money, and pretty soon, dat boy dere, he still don' got no food and no bed."

"I want my grandbaby to get an education like other children." Tía Pilar touched Amaia's stomach—she was six months pregnant with her first child.

"Dat baby can get any education he want."

"I send him to England for education," said Tía Pilar proudly. "I don't worry about him. I worry about all the other children."

"You just worry 'bout your own. More people do dat, den we got no problem."

Having stayed on the sidelines, I cared more about finding a convenient place to end the evening than about interjecting my own opinion. I found no good time. Instead, I yawned mightily and hoped that Tía Pilar noticed.

"Tiene sueño?"

"Yes, I'm tired, Tía Pilar."

Hopping up from her seat, she grabbed me by the arm and led me—no, dragged me—down the hall to the bedroom.

The sheets and blankets of my bed had been ironed and folded back in a triangle. I lay down, my head on a sponge pillow, and listened through the door to muffled voices, softer, then louder, higher, then lower, first from Dad, then from Tía Pilar, back and forth, well into the early-morning hours. I didn't know their subjects or care to know. The arguments didn't matter and not one of them was new. Neither would make progress on the other, no mind would turn, no opinion would change.

What mattered was each soaking up the timbre and rhythm of the other. Memory derived from many guises, many forms. Long after points of contention had faded and the body had turned to dust, the voice resonated in the ear as profoundly as faces collected in the mind.

The two in the kitchen sounded like brother and sister fighting for the sake of fighting. That's what siblings do.

I finally fell asleep to the harmony of their beautiful disagreements.

# 16

I enrolled at age nine in the Big "E" 4-H Club as a natural extension of the various sheep activities of our farm—feeding, birthing, shearing, and butchering. I loathed joining up, never really enjoying the beasts or caring enough to show them in front of a live audience. But my older sister had signed up two years before and earned top honors with her lamb named Barbie. It gave Dad the adulation that he secretly craved, addicting him like an opium eater, swelling his heart and widening his face.

I sensed that craving and swelling and widening and knew then of his happiness and wanted to be part of it—for his sake, yes, but selfishly, also for my sake. I wanted to cause his joy and have him know that I brought happiness to him. Then I hoped for his pride, heaps of it, to sate my own craving for attention and acceptance, as any son might, and reasoned that attention meant approval and approval meant love. The loathing I felt by joining up mattered not at all.

By early spring, Dad selected a lamb that I dubbed "the Chosen One" because of how lavishly Dad treated it from day one—extra milk from a bottle, extra grain from the palm, extra hay from a bag. He praised the beast, whispered in its ear and petted its head. I mimicked his actions, believing that the imitation endeared me to him, that praise of the lamb drew Dad's praise of me.

The lamb developed an ego, prancing around with a higher head and stomping its feet at threats, like poor Tramp, our new dog after Lady, who efficiently corralled the other sheep but stepped back from the Chosen One, sensing Dad's partiality for it. Dad liked arrogant sheep. "Little pride goes long way," he often said.

The Chosen One didn't impress me, nor did I appease it like Tramp did. I saw it as a tool to gain Dad's hard-won affections, which he stoically withheld, not maliciously but naturally, like so many Basque men who covered feeling in layers of stony armor. But the tool had no instructions. I had no plan for transferring or converting Dad's whispers or palms of grain or extra hay into loving endearments for me, and so the lamb, though my only mechanism, became equally an obstacle, at once pernicious and essential.

I resented the animal. I gave him a new name—*It*. No name other than a simple, neutral, noncommittal pronoun could capture my bitterness, jealousy, and contempt, or bring down the soaring ego of this shit-wallowing four-legger destined for the dinner table.

As much power as *It* had over Dad and Tramp, I relished knowing what the future held for him. I had watched a year before a macabre scene unfold in our field. Until then, I had had little idea what sheep endured at the hands of their shepherds, but now I felt a small glee for the misery in store, a dark schaden-freude that swamped my soul.

On a Saturday morning in May, Dad gathered Basque friends in the field—Chapo, Domingo, Juanito, and Alfonso. They started with the two-month-old ewes, flipping each one on its back to expose the underbelly, and with a pocketknife hacking off the wriggling tail, leaving a one-inch bloody stump. Each got a shot of penicillin to ward off infection and then was sent on wobbly legs back to the field, dripping blood from its hindquarters. Months after the stump healed, it flitted back and forth, imitating the wiggles of a longer tail. I thought of the man missing a leg who still felt the itch in his foot.

As a proud, egotistical male, *It* endured the hacking without a bleat—strong, sheeply, arrogant. I felt no remorse when the knife blade lopped off the eight inches. But on this day, *It* would lose more than a tail; he would become a nut-less wonder, a *castrado* with a high-pitched bleat and a diminished libido.

Alfonso hacked the tails and performed most of the castrations, but after *It*'s tail fell, Dad took over the ball-busting ceremony. As I stood transfixed, he serialized the three steps that still echo in my cranium. At the time, I found my own legs crossing in solidarity with the lamb's vulnerability.

"You cut first," Dad said. With the lamb on its back and Alfonso holding the hind legs apart, Dad made a two-inch incision with his pocketknife across the scrotum sack.

"Den you bite." He plunged his face into the sheep's groin, catching the tes-ticles between his teeth and pulling his head up and back. The testicles fol-lowed in a long stream as *It* squealed like a prepubescent girl. Swirling with pink blood like a candy cane, white-hot gonads dangled from Dad's lips and swung below his chin. He unclenched his teeth and dropped the male-meat into a bucket at his side.

"Den you pull," he said belatedly, catching his breath. "Cut—bite—pull," he repeated formulaically. "Dat's all dere is to it."

He wiped his mouth with the back of his hand while Alfonso administered a penicillin shot and then released the animal. *It* stood dazed and then limped with less pride to the dispirited tail-less, ball-less herd.

Nothing repulsed me as much as this teeth-testicle extraction. Years later, sitting across a table from less than scrupulous executives, or politicians here and abroad, or other dark representatives of society, my mind occasionally wandered to the sight of *It* upturned in the field and his nuts dangling from Dad's lips. I then muscled up to the table and held my ground and struck a deal that cut, bit, and pulled, leaving the sordid men to skulk away dispirited and justifiably deflated. Ego in my midst attracted the memory of *It*'s diminution.

But any vindication from the moment was short-lived. My chores regarding *It* began immediately and once again I found myself subordinated in his midst.

From a length of nylon rope, Dad made a halter that fit on *It*'s black face. Naturally, as I pulled the rope, *It* resisted.

"Please move," I asked politely.

I felt *It* reply, "Fuck you," and he dug hooves in the mud and manure.

I reached behind *It* and squeezed his tender stump of a tail, causing him to bleat and groan and lurch forward.

"Thank you," I responded.

"Fuck off!" *It* came back.

In late June, Dad sheared *It*, careful not to nick the flesh. Red spots popped up from the mangling of engorged ticks while others crept to deeper cover near the buttocks or legs. Dad picked them off and squished them. Standing *It* up, he used hand clippers to even the shave and brush the sides. Other lambs, including the larger, older sheep, were sheared in fifteen minutes, but *It* received an hour of Dad's precious time. My resentment built and jealousy came in waves.

With head high, *It* seemed to bleat, "I am Lamb of God."

I thought in retort, "No, you are rack of lamb."

Once *It* had been halter-broken, Dad started him on a high-protein diet of grain and oats, carrots from the garden for fiber, and castor oil in milk or water to fatten its loins, broaden its back, and fill out its ribs. Every other week, he weighed *It* and mentally charted the progress. When we checked in at the fairgrounds in August, *It* had to weigh ideally 120 pounds—any less and we sacrificed dollars per pound, any more and we gave away extra meat. Rarely did any lamb hit the mark exactly.

*It* grew as a clear standout among the other lambs—a few inches taller, a shinier black face, a broader back.

With the added food, he needed exercise to widen his upper legs, tone the muscle, and make him stocky around the shoulders. I dreaded the nightly walks with this arrogant creature from our house, up a desolate street, through sagebrush, and finally to a cattle guard. Four trips up and back made one mile.

A test of wills often ensued. *It* stopped—simply refused to budge—and no amount of tail tapping or tail twisting would change his feeble mind.

"Move! Damn it!" I demanded in frustration.

*It* looked to reply, "Fuck off!"

Pulling the rope with all I had, I moved *It* a foot. Then tying the rope to my belt, I used my legs for greater leverage.

"What do you want?" I yelled, nearly in tears.

"Suffer, little man!" *It* intimated and lay in the road, spitefully appearing to chew invisible grass.

My face reddened. I had no recourse but to sit next to this repulsive grass-eating herbivore and wait until *It* yearned again for the barn over the luxury of rest. The epitome of sloth for thirty minutes, he finally rose, bleated twice, and double-timed back home. I often caught Dad laughing at the stalemate and felt small and less favored and jealous. I imagined a chain saw tearing through *It*'s oily wool.

In the days before the Elko County Fair, I had to bathe the beast. I wanted to use Clorox, but Dad said the chemicals would scald *It*'s skin and tear off the wool. He gave me instead a special soap that lathered into thick foam and cleaned while tenderly bleaching.

Using our garden hose, I sensed *It* say, "The water's freezing."

My mental retort was, "I know, mutton-to-be," and I sprayed his face.

"Try this, chubby bastard," *It* said, shaking like a dog and drenching me in soapy water that burned my skin.

*It* contemptuously added, "Learned that trick from the dog."

Dad had me paint *It*'s hooves with black shoe polish like lumps of shiny obsidian. Later I used curry combs and carding brushes to pouf up the wool like cotton "to make him look good," as Dad said, as if *It* needed an ego boost.

Had I had the chance to deliver this empty-scrotum bleater to the meat grinder, I would have gladly paid a full year's allowance. But my yearning and aching for Dad's joy told me to shine the wool like new-fallen snow, and to make the black hooves gleam like a cat's eye, and then his praise would come.

Dad affixed burlap covering to keep *It* clean, as he had for the living lamb, so many years before, but he said nothing else about the lamb's appearance. I wished for a can of tar to unfluff the wool.

Driving to the fairgrounds, I sat in the back of Dad's pickup holding the halter to keep *It* from jumping the side and hanging. Oh, dare to dream!

At weigh-in, *It* entered a metal chute as two officials tapped a balance on a scale centimeter by centimeter and then yelled out, "120 pounds."

"I am perfection," I felt *It* say.

A rash of hushed whispers welled up from the ranchers who sat in bleachers sizing up their competition. Dad beamed with pride. I saw the look and knew it. The ears went up a few centimeters, a sparkle dazzled in the eyes, his smile broadened, and his hands folded prayerfully. None of this was for me.

"Why don't you get in the chute, chubby? Let's weigh you," insinuated *It*.

"You'll be lighter and more perfect without wool," I contended. "In a week you'll be a shishkabob, but I'll be chubby, pleasantly happy, and—did I mention—alive."

The next day was show day. To rival my Fourth of July Basque costume, my parents now dressed me in green pants, white shirt, and a green clip-on with 4-h emblazoned at the center.

*It* inferred, "You're a fat leprechaun. I'm embarrassed for you."

I had no retort.

In my back pocket, I carried a curry comb in case *It*'s appearance poufed insufficiently at a critical time when the judge expected cotton-like wool. I never had cause—not once—to improve *It*'s appearance for a judge's sake and the curry comb stayed in my pocket.

The rules prevented me or any of my thirty-four competitors from using a halter to lead an animal into the show ring. We had to drag the animal by the thin skin under the nose. The first competition was not for showmanship; it considered only the condition of the animal, its musculature, and its capacity for yielding high-quality lamb chops.

The judge circled us, touched each lamb, measured the leg and the width of the back. Then he arranged the beasts from first to last, awarding a grand champion, a reserve champion, and several blue, red, and white ribbons.

He instructed me to go to the front of the line, and then made a few admiring remarks over a microphone to the large audience. A young lady passed me and laid a purple and gold Grand Champion ribbon across *It*'s cotton-like back.

"I am king of the world!" glowed *It*. "The fine little miss placed the ribbon on my back, not in your pudgy hand. You are nothing without me."

"Floppy-eared, ball-less rump roast!" I retorted and then waved at Dad as he beamed in the bleachers. Strange, my ambivalence. The lamb outdid all others, a testament to Dad's knowledge and care of sheep, but the prize did not belong to me, only to Dad and to the lamb, and again I wallowed in isolation, devoid of love, looking from outside in at a growing bond between Dad and the sheep.

Next day, a second competition of showmanship rated the boy and not the lamb. I led *It* into the ring and instantly a silent declaration came from him, a defiant pride. "I am the worthiest lamb—nay, sheep—on these whole grounds, and you, my young sniveling idiot, have no power over me. I cannot be shamed, for I have a ribbon to show my worth, but you, little urchin, have no ribbon, no talent, and no control over a sheep of my high distinction and breeding. Your glory or shame lies in my well-manicured hooves. I am the Chosen One."

"You behave, or else," I said weakly with trepidation.

The rules for showmanship were difficult. The lamb had to remain between you and the judge at all times. The legs had to be squared, a feat equivalent to solving a Rubik's Cube—as one leg moved back, another jerked forward.

The judge asked us to walk our lambs around the ring to show that we controlled our beasts and the beasts didn't control us. I knew what *It* thought of this preposterous notion. But mysteriously, he cooperated, walking when tugged and standing with squared legs and broad back when at rest.

"So far, so good," I congratulated myself.

I fared well due to a spate of unfortunate accidents among my peers. One lamb bumped another, then another, like dominoes, un-squaring legs and riling the bunch. But I and *It* stood awkwardly apart from the others—most likely by *It's* design, not mine—so the chain broke with me.

The judge instructed me to go to the head of the line again as he made his way to the microphone. The chance of a lightning strike was a million to one, but it struck somewhere on something. Why not for me now? I had won in spite of my own limited skills. God existed and He smiled on me now. I turned to Dad and saw the beam—ears up, eyes aglow, smile wide, hands folded—all of it for me, not the lamb, not the tool, only for me, and I felt good and whole and warm and knew of a father's love.

Sensing a pause as the judge fiddled with the microphone, *It* declared, "Watch this, you foolish little peon," and reared on his hind legs, jerked free, and raced around the ring. I stood paralyzed.

"Oh, Lord in Heaven," I prayed, "please strike this beast down and me next. End my humiliation before this audience of laughing hyenas."

The judge set down the microphone, caught *It*, and then said, "Sonny, to the back of the line."

I went to the end, holding back tears of shame for Mom and Dad watching from the crowd. I received a red ribbon, bottom of the barrel. All expectations tumbled down and the goodness and warmth and love evaporated and though I dared not look at Dad directly, I saw him from the corner of my eye—the beam had gone.

"Now 'Sonny,'" *It* mocked, "who's in control now? Who is the *It*? You're not worth one of my high protein turds and now we have ribbons to prove it, 'Sonny.'"

"I will use your pelt as a rug, you mongrel mammal," I raged.

In the morning on the last day of the Elko Fair, I escorted *It* into the ring before a massive crowd and a fiery auctioneer.

"Here's the Grand Champion lamb, ladies and gentlemen," said the auctioneer. "The very best we got."

"Hear that, kid? 'The very best,'" I sensed *It* chortling as the alpha lamb.

"Let's start the bidding," continued the auctioneer. "Do I hear 10 dollars . . . I got 10, now 12, 12, 12, do I got 12 . . . I got 12, now 15 dollars, 15, 15, now 18, 18, 18, now 18, 18 . . . got 18 . . . 22 dollars . . . 22, 22, 22 dollars . . . now I got 22, 27 how 'bout 27, 27 dollars.

"Now, ladies and gentlemen"—the auctioneer paused, catching his breath—"they don't get any better than this one. You're going to be sorry if you let this one get by."

"'They'll be sorry,'" I felt *It* say. "Told you, urchin. I'm cock of the walk."

"You'll make great lining for a winter coat," I mentally retorted.

Another hand shot up as the bidding resumed.

"27 dollars, 27 . . . I got 27, now 30, 30, do I have 30, yes 30 . . . and 32 now, 32 . . . going once . . ."

"$32.50," came a yell from the crowd.

"I got $32.50 . . . going once . . . twice . . . sold . . . for 32 dollars and 50 cents a pound." And he slammed a gavel down on his bench.

The crowd roared. *It* set a new record for a single lamb at the Elko County Fair, one that the ranchers grumbled about, fearing that the thirty-four lambs that followed would suffer commensurately low bids. I didn't care either way. The record-setting result had little to do with me. I stood in one place, gazing at the audience, hoping for an end to the proceedings as my humiliation lingered from the day before.

At 4 PM, Dad met me at the stall to halter *It* one last time. From *It*'s ear tag, he hung the purple and gold ribbon proclaiming Grand Champion status. I walked the lamb outside to a large semi already filling with cattle and sheep. I led *It* to the ramp, pulled off the halter, and whispered in his floppy black ear, "Enjoy your final ride," and then twisted the tail for one last lurch into the truck.

Looking back, *It* noticeably bleated, "Fuck off!"

Gathering the rope in my hands, I stood with Mom and Dad to watch several men seal the truck, get in the cab, and drive away.

"Dat was a good lamb," Dad said.

"Yes, he was," agreed Mom.

Mom put her arm around me, thinking I too felt sadness. Looking around the truck at young people sobbing, I felt guilt for not crying too, but a greater sense of ambivalence—a relief from months of warring with the beast, but a disappointment, too, that the mechanism through which Dad experienced such joy had been taken from me and my chance of attracting his praise had gone with it.

The reprieve lasted until March of the new year, when Dad made another selection, a second Chosen One, a female, whom I loathsomely dubbed *You*. The warring began anew, and so did my chance with Dad.

# 17

Tía Pilar persuaded us to stay another night with her and Tío Pedro. We had no arguments to countermand her forceful reasoning. If chastity had kept her from embracing the convent, she nonetheless had mastered the subtle power of guilt as a mature, well-practiced Catholic. She combined the best parts of Sister Mary Kathleen and Sister Dennis, at once stern, disciplined, and certain, while simultaneously kind, warm, and willing to hug.

We left Mondragón in the Subaru to find Tío Joakin, Dad's younger brother, who still lived in Gizaburuaga, their childhood home.

"Where is this place?" I asked Dad.

"You jus' go up dat road dere. I know where to go. Dat's where I born."

The town, on a good day, had a population of ten, assuming none of its inhabitants had died that day or driven to Lekeitio for groceries.

"You not find dis on no map."

Fearing we might miss it, I typed the town phonetically into the GPS.

"You no find it dere."

"It can't hurt to try."

"Nobody knows how to get dere. I do. You got to do one secret turn."

"I found it, Dad."

"Bullshit!"

"Here, look." As I showed him the route, the British female voice began her directions.

"I be a sonofabitch."

"It's not secret anymore," I said, poking at him. Admittedly, though, the secret turn of which Dad spoke was a 180-degree twist to the right up a steep mud hill.

"Who the hell lives up here?"

"Mountain goats," he shot back.

Having been designed apparently for a wagon pulled by a single horse, the road had little room for the Subaru. I feared that one of the ten residents might need to pass and we'd find ourselves at a severe impasse.

"You were born here?"

"Yes. Up top dat hill. Dere's one house up dere. I born up dere." The hill seemed deserted, showing no sign of structures, roads, or any human existence. It rose like an island in the clouds.

"Are you sure you lived up there?"

" 'Course, I'm sure!" he yelled back and hit me in the arm.

"Do you want to go see it?"

"No. No." He wagged his finger.

"Why not? We're so close."

"No, I 'member how I want to 'member it."

"It's not a problem. We can find a way up there."

"No, I don' want to go."

"It's no trouble, really."

"If I go see it—see if you understand me—den I can't 'member it except how I see it now. Den I can't 'member no more how I 'member it from long time ago."

"Can't you remember it both ways?"

"No. Can't. You do dat, den how I 'member before, it goes away."

"You mean that the new memory crowds out the old memory? Sometimes that's a good thing."

"Only if de new one better."

"That makes sense," I agreed. "You think your old memory is better?"

"Dere's not a day go by dat I don' think of dat place, about Momma and

Daddy." He pointed again to the hill and the hidden house shrouded among pines or wiped away by man and nature years ago. "I dream 'bout it every night. I don' 'member anything like I 'member dat place."

"Let me know if you change your mind. We can go up there anytime."

I worried about making a promise I couldn't keep. Horses and wagons could go where Subarus dared not tread. I also worried that if we made the trek we'd find the old house gone, with thick forest growing where rice pudding once sat on a table or brothers and sisters once slept in beds or a father once loaded wood grudgingly for Franco's soldiers. Visiting a childhood haunt had an equal chance of softly reinforcing an old memory or violently burning it to ashes. I hoped that I didn't have to risk the latter while I promised the former.

"Where do I go now?"

"What? Dat machine, it lost?" he said smugly, nodding at the GPS.

"I think it is, Dad."

"You jus' keepa goin' straight."

The land flattened into a valley of elms, spaced five feet apart, lining the road, and staggered in nearly perfect diagonals, one just aside the other like a column of disciplined soldiers standing at attention. The centurions stretched with deep precision on either side and slunk their way over the humps of mountains marching for miles beyond. Rain drizzled and grayness smeared over everything.

"Now you follow along here," he instructed as the GPS whirled and the British female voice kept repeating, "Rerouting."

"Dat's one piece of shit," Dad commented. "Jus' throw dat out de window."

"It gets confused sometimes," I said.

"It get confused. Den you throw out de window."

"You get confused too."

"But I don' fit through de window." He chuckled at his own quick wit.

"Over dere." He pointed. "Dat's Joakin's place."

Out of the woods, a small farmhouse popped up, completely out of place. It appeared at any moment that nature might swallow it whole and wipe away any hint of a human footprint. A dog slept in front next to a pile of wood, and it didn't move as we drove up. It looked old and could have been dead.

I had met Tío Joakin only once, and it had been a highly regrettable experience. After college, I had backpacked through nine European countries with a high school friend of mine, Jonathan. While in Spain, we visited my relatives, who filled our bellies, chauffeured and entertained us, and bedded us down for several nights. But when we pulled up to Tío Joakin's house, he came out, his oily white hair matted from a nap, and like a hibernating bear yawned and growled in such a way that it reminded me of Juanito's hyena cackle from the Blue Jay Bar. Having never met him, I had expected from him a handshake, a hug, a cheek-to-cheek kiss, and a quick question about Dad's welfare. Instead, he barreled toward me like a linebacker and grabbed my leg, knocking me to the ground. I lay splayed atop my backpack, helpless like an overturned turtle while he guffawed over me and kicked me in the legs and side with his big black boots.

Jonathan had stood back, laughing nervously, and asked me later if I had been adopted, or if Tío Joakin had been adopted, believing that my uncle and I could never have sprung from similar strands of DNA.

Mindful of that encounter, I stood by the Subaru in the rain as Dad knocked and Tío Joakin answered the door. For three minutes, the two of them cussed and yelled with baritone timbres louder and louder, and finally, after a remarkable display of degenerate profanity, embraced and squeezed hard until their faces reddened and purpled and the veins on their necks swelled to a condition of pre–cardiac arrest. I remained near the car and bore witness to this bizarre ritual of Basque machismo unmitigated by American congeniality.

Waved inside, I followed Dad, Joakin, and my Tía Miren, a square and sturdy farmer's wife decked out in ankle-length skirt, thick-soled shoes, sweater, and apron. She had zero tolerance for the frills or feminine affectations customary in urban living. In fact, she probably knew nothing about lace collars, makeup, or heels. She fit the role of a hard country woman.

The house was dark, lacking electricity, and felt damp and cold. A rifle stood upright in the corner by the front door. In the kitchen, Tía Miren moved an iron ring from the stove with a hook and piled wood inside. From a few meager cupboards, she brought out half a loaf of stale bread, a bottle of wine, and a block of homemade unpasteurized goat cheese. She pressed it on a dirty plate and set it on the kitchen table.

Dad and Tío Joakin yelled at each other in animated yet friendly conversation. Tía Miren stood by the stove quietly, with arms folded, continually moving and restoring the iron ring with the hook, ensuring that the embers turned and the stove churned out heat.

Tío Joakin was a burly, thick, muscular man who rose five feet five inches while wearing his black boots. When I had seen him twenty years before with

Jonathan, he had had five teeth (that I could count), but now that number had declined to three, and I wondered what had happened to the other two.

He also had a new feature—a pointer finger gone terribly askew. I thought at first that he suffered from severe arthritis, but I learned that he had accidentally sawed it off while cutting trees, and then plucked it from the ground, wiped off the sawdust, and brought it back to the house, where he and Tía Miren reattached it with her sewing kit. Unfortunately, neither of them had any medical training or tools, so in the dim afternoon light of their kitchen, they ended up sewing the finger on crooked. It leaned at a grizzly angle starting at the second knuckle.

Dad and Tío Joakin became more animated in their conversation, and I noted a profound seriousness come over Dad's face.

"I won't talk to her no more!" Joakin said.

"Got to sometime," replied Dad.

"Not after that. She only wanted money. I told her last time I saw her, and she didn't want to see me either."

"Joakin, dat's your sister."

"Not my sister."

"Whether you like it or not," Dad said.

"That was Momma and Daddy's ranch," Joakin said. "They wanted us to keep it. And she wanted the money. Told us to move on. You got to hold to those things. Those things important. Too many disappearing, all of them. If you don't, then it dies and you die and the kids, they have nothing. Pretty soon, nothing left of anything."

My grandparents had bequeathed a ranch in equal shares to their children with instructions to run the property as a lumber producer or to sell it and share the proceeds equally. The eight brothers and sisters had split on the decision—some, like Tío Joakin, wanting to operate the ranch as a lumber producer in nostalgic honor of their parents and some preferring to sell immediately. Indecision had produced arguments, then rifts, and finally, a permanent silence between some siblings, especially Tío Joakin and Tía Juanita, who convalesced with Tía Anita seven miles away in Lekeitio's nursing home.

The feud took new form when a fire erupted on the property, burning half the elms and pines, and reducing the overall value of the land. The brothers and sisters attributed this unfortunate turn of fate to a godly act of retribution inflicted on them for their obstinate behavior. Ironically, each side presumed that God had intervened to punish the stance of the other. In the end, the eight sold the property for half its original value and went their separate ways. Dad had remained indifferent in the decision, opting to cast his vote with the majority. But hard feelings remained and silence between several of the brothers and sisters persists to this day.

"I seen Anita and Juanita few days ago," Dad said. "Dey all crippled up. Anita, she don' 'member much, and Juanita, she can't walk by herself. You go see dem. Dey jus' over the hill, not too far away."

"I don't need to see them," said Joakin. He folded his arms.

"Would be nice," said Dad.

"Hell no!" yelled Joakin. He raised the crooked pointer, and while his hand gestured to Dad, the finger angled ghoulishly toward me. I thought of God's finger outstretched to Adam in the Sistine Chapel, and how Tío Joakin's finger might have modeled perfectly for the same scene had Picasso been the artist and not Michelangelo.

"You goin' to die out here and never talk to dem?" asked Dad.

Joakin folded his arms. "Why not?"

"You go see dem. Make new memories," Dad scolded. His own finger came out, and it wagged straight and purposeful.

I had seen Dad the worker, Dad the husband, Dad the protector, Dad the bold, Dad the competitor. But not until now had I seen Dad the big brother. It reminded me of similar finger-wagging moments between me and Amy, my younger sister.

Tía Miren, to break the growing tension, sliced a piece of goat cheese for me. I choked it down, wondering what regimen of antibiotics might be needed and for what duration to stave off the swarming bacteria.

Tío Joakin poured wine for me, him, and Dad. Standing and raising his glass, he said, "To my brother and his son, and to your wife and your daughters, and to the whole family. Salud."

We drank.

Wine flowed for two hours until the bottle was emptied and the cheese slab whittled to a quarter its original size. Tío Joakin hugged me and didn't grab my leg, and Tía Miren kissed me on both cheeks. Dad and his brother squeezed each other at the door, and by their grip, it appeared that each hoped to collapse the rib cage of the other.

As we idled back through the soldier elms, Dad said, "I miss him."

"It's good you saw him. Believe it or not, I'm glad I saw him too."

"Too bad I don' see him every day. Den we could 'member each other better."

"You could move back to Spain," I quipped.

"Hell no!"

I chuckled.

The rain beat on the windshield.

The British female said, "Rerouting."

# 18

"Someday, dese sheep, dey belong to you, but won't be hundred sheep; you goin' to have thousand or more. Dat's how dis country is, if you work hard enough."

These words greeted me weekly as I grew up. Dad placed his limitations at a hundred sheep, the size of our herd. Given a second lifetime lived through me, Dad allowed his ambition to expand tenfold, perhaps because he had more faith in his children, or because half his life was chewed up by coming to America, working for others, gaining citizenship, and learning the language.

The words came so often that I learned them as rote, and eventually my expectations aligned with his, one and the same. I saw myself a sheepherder, or as Dad described the profession, a rancher. The difference between the two was ownership.

At dinner it came. "You goin' to own one ranch someday. You mark my word." And it followed at breakfast. "You got to learn 'bout runnin' a ranch."

He told friends, relatives, anyone who cared to listen. At Basque festivals, he reinforced the message among a dense audience of red-sashed, beret-wearing men who, I imagined, had similar dreams for their sons.

Just as I never doubted God's Book of Names, I never doubted Dad's rendition of my destiny. In bed at night, I pictured myself in my mind's eye, herding, gutting, moving sprinklers, fixing fences, building barns, taking care of all of Dad's daily chores. I had little knowledge of how a sheepherder differed from a rancher, though knowing there was a gap, I filled it with more of the same—more herding, gutting, sprinklers, fences, barns.

I went with Dad to Paris Ranch near Jiggs to help shear sheep, a job Dad did on weekends for extra money, ten to fifteen dollars per head. Dad bound three legs and moved the shears along the sheep's underbelly, and I held the fourth leg while a ranch hand supervised.

"Can your boy shear sheep?" asked the chubby fellow with a bulbous belly flopping over his buckle.

Dad powered off the shears. Breathing heavy, he said, "He don' need to."

"Why's that?" asked the butter-belly.

"Someday, he goin' to own one ranch and we both goin' to work for him."

So the pressure mounted. I fully expected a life on the range, roaming Nevada's mountains, lambing in spring, yanking their gonads with my teeth, shearing wool, enduring summer heat, and hunkering down to pass the winter. I even expected one day to slash the throat, crack the spine, and butcher the beasts for meat. Dad's words resonated morning and night in my head. No others squeezed in—until the third grade.

Marta Moschetti, a silver-haired peach of a lady, asked in class a rather pernicious question—"What do you want to be when you grow up?"

Around the room, my classmates said, "Fireman" or "Doctor" or "Nurse" or some other conventional answer.

"I'm going to be a rancher," I told her.

"What does a rancher do?" Her soft voice matched a kind face of warmth.

"Someone who herds sheep, lots of sheep, more than a hundred."

"Have you always wanted to be a rancher?" she asked.

I thought a moment. "Yes."

"Have you ever wanted to be anything else?"

I thought again. "No, just a rancher."

"I see."

"What about you?" Mrs. Moschetti pointed at Glenna, a petite auburn-haired girl in the second row. "Have you always wanted to be a nurse?"

"Pretty much," she said through a smile of discolored teeth. "I like to ride horses, so I'd do that too. Yeah, I think that's what I want to do, is ride horses."

"And you, Stacey." The long pointer roamed the room. "Did you always want to play the guitar?"

"I think driving racecars would be a blast," she said, trying to hide her gum.

"Racecars? Quite daring," said Mrs. Moschetti. "Please place your gum in the trash can."

"What about you, Brian?" The pointer cast about. "Did you always want to be a fireman?"

"Well, that and a train engineer," he said. People chuckled. Brian was the nose-picker whom everyone tormented to satisfy child cruelty.

"That's enough, everyone," said Mrs. Moschetti, and we hushed instantly.

Her pointer came back to me. "So, everyone has wanted to be many things. Are you still so sure about being a rancher?"

Eyes were on me and a hot blush burned my white cheeks. I didn't say anything.

"Let me ask you this," she said. "If you couldn't be a rancher—let's say they were no longer allowed—what would you like to be?"

The whole class turned in their chairs, sensing that my answer was somehow critical. Silence weighed heavily and guilt welled up in me.

"If I c-c-c-couldn't be a r-r-r-rancher," I stammered, "well . . . I would be a United States senator."

Mrs. Moschetti smiled. "Could you tell the class what a United States senator is?"

"Someone who makes laws for the people," I replied smartly. I had learned about U.S. senators from one of our *Weekly Readers*.

Then Brian said, "I'd like to be one of them."

Ignoring him and pointing at me, Mrs. Moschetti said, "Now you can be a rancher or a United States Senator, and maybe next week, you might want to be something else too."

She held her piercing stare until I squirmed in my chair. "Listen up, all of you." She clapped her hands twice for attention. "You can be anything you want to be if you work hard enough. Just believe in yourself."

Mrs. Moschetti gave us love and light and inspiration, all braided into a grandmotherly figure. We minded and revered her, learning what we had to learn because she wanted us to learn it. Like all teachers, she had the right to send us to the principal's office to see Mr. Ridgeway, at the time a scary mustached man, who had tacit approval from all parents to pull a paddle from his wall or a belt from his waist and enforce discipline. But no one from our class ever went because Mrs. Moschetti's soft voice and velvet glove kept us in check.

The more I thought of that day in class, the more I realized that a line of demarcation had been drawn between Dad's interests and mine. Until then, they had been interchangeable. But Mrs. Moschetti had slid the finest of silken threads between the two and allowed me the luxury of considering other options.

Over dinner and at breakfast, Dad continued with his recitations. "Pretty soon, not too far now, you gonna own a ranch and have a thousand head, maybe two thousand, or more." In that moment, I thought, *Or maybe I will be something else!*

A guilty feeling came over me and I tucked the thought away. But it returned whenever Dad made another proclamation, and each time I pushed it down, it grew stronger and stayed out longer no matter how I struggled to suppress it.

When I reached junior high, the number of sheep multiplied from a thousand to two thousand to ten thousand. I couldn't fathom a typical day. No amount of daylight offered ample time for so many sheep or barns or sprinklers. The dream was falling apart.

The thought came out in the eighth grade with high school on the horizon and I couldn't suppress it: *Or maybe I will be something else!*

The sentiment overwhelmed being a rancher. The silken thread, once inserted by Mrs. Moschetti, had widened between Dad's interests and mine, like the smallest river, given enough time, eroded a landscape into a mighty canyon.

Stepping over that line with Dad's ambitions on one side and mine on the other, I gave up clarity of purpose in favor of an unknown future. But if Glenna could ride horses, Stacey race cars, and Brian drive trains, I expected that some other destiny could lie in wait for me.

What concerned me more than the unknown was the fear of hurting Dad. For years, he had told me and others, anyone who would listen, about the ranch that I would own and operate, a great establishment in the mountains of Nevada, teeming with untold thousands of sheep and cattle. A lifetime of energy had been invested in this dream. How could anyone, especially a son, dash such a hope? If I crossed the line, as conscience compelled me, it meant leaving him forever behind with his hundred sheep.

I wrestled with how to tell him or when. After he had worked twelve or fourteen hours? In the early morning as he scrambled out the door? Or while Mom and my sisters were hanging around? No time seemed like the right time.

We had to be alone, someplace where we could talk without interruption. I expected the conversation to be drawn out, full of countermanded hopes and dreams, anger and raised voices, with me standing my ground in the face of uncertainty and fear.

But when?

On a clear Saturday afternoon, in the summer after my eighth-grade year, with sunshine burning the desert sagebrush, Dad came to the house and said, "I need your help." He didn't say for what, but I figured for barn fixing.

No one else could have discerned this fact, but I knew. If Dad wanted help butchering, he inched his head close to mine and whispered, "I need your help," a message that said, "We have death to do."

Help with a fence, on the other hand, showed on his face. By the time he came to the house and said, "I need your help," he had already worked at the fence for an hour, sweating and breathing heavy, and decided that he couldn't do it alone.

But on this day, when he said, "I need your help," the rapid stride of his short legs, the determination of his wrinkled forehead, and no sign of sweat suggested a larger plan in the offing, like barn building.

In the garage, we each grabbed a hammer and a Folgers can of nails, and I followed him to the barn, a makeshift structure of plywood from the city dump or the trash heap at the local lumber company. The roof had overlapping sheets of metal with sharp edges. Nothing fit quite right, making the thing appear like a patchwork quilt in all shapes, sizes, and colors.

We hopped from hay bale to hay bale like stepping-stones to get on the tin roof. Heat radiated off the metal and raised the temperature fifteen degrees. A scattering of sprinkler clicks and bleating ewes broke the smothering dry air.

Dad pulled a nail from the can and set it in place. Before the hammer struck, I blurted out, "Dad, I want to leave Elko and go to college."

He paused—hammer in midair.

Then he struck three times to make the nail flush against the tin.

But he said nothing.

I took up my hammer and pounded nails with him, one after the other. We made our way across the hot tin roof with beads of sweat desperately trying to keep us cool. The silence between us and the stillness of the air made me uncomfortable and anxious and sick to my stomach. I heard drops of perspiration hit the metal sheets and sizzle to oblivion.

Another nail.

Pounding.

One inch back.

Sweat and sizzle.

Silence.

Another nail.

More pounding.

One inch back.

Sweat and sizzle.

Insufferable silence.

One thought burned in my mind. I had hurt Dad's feelings, dashed his dreams. Nothing I could say or do could turn back the clock before the hammer strike.

I smashed my thumb and it bled. I justified the pain as divine retribution for my selfish and wicked disregard for Dad's feelings and humble nature. I had to finish the task, part from Dad, and try to reconcile my personal ambition with his greater sacrifices and dreams. I had to find a way to weld the before and after and restore the timeline. This was one of those heavy moments.

After two hours, with few nails left in our coffee cans, Dad raised to one knee and rested the hammer on his thigh. I took out the remaining nails without looking up or locking eyes. He took off his hat, ran his hands through thinning hair, scratched his whiskers, and said, "It good idea you go to college."

Then with Folgers can in hand, he stepped down the bales and made his way home.

I watched him get smaller as he crossed the field into the house. I dangled my legs off the edge of the barn. Below in the sheep's trough, long-legged bugs skimmed the surface, bumped the edges of their universe, and reversed. I looked out over our acreage as I had a thousand times before, at ewes tearing up shoots of summer grass and sagebrush stretching over rolling hills. The lonely elm in the corner after so many lightning strikes stood a little taller, upright and strong. I listened to clicking sprinklers all around, smelled hot manure and the scent of milkweed. The sun seared the horizon, turning wispy clouds into streaks of cotton candy.

I admired everything around me, so familiar, yet so new, all for the first time.

# 19

Southeast of Elko on Lamoille Highway, no more than seven miles, the road summits and reveals a majestic panorama of purple-hued mountains called the Nevada Rubies, not unlike the Pyrenees of Spain. Farther down, the road reaches the town of Spring Creek, and then turning deeper south into rolling hills and sagebrush, at a sign that says JIGGS, 35 MILES, the pavement goes from oil to gravel to dirt. In summer, dust rises six feet behind the truck and in winter, gravel and dirt make the road nearly impassable.

Along the route are splintered fences that once corralled hundreds of thousands of sheep and cattle, but that was more than three-quarters of a century ago.

Only shards of energetic Western life remained—a few head of cattle, a mere shadow of past glories; random goats flocking like geese on open prairies; sheep and coyotes keeping each other in balance; and barns and homes collapsing under the weight of seventy-five winters.

"Dis hard country," Dad said.

"You bet," Jess agreed with the same baritone I had heard at Basque festivals in my youth.

I didn't have to be there to know they were right—no trees for shade, no shelter from blizzards, great distance between water holes, bobcats and coyotes, rattlesnakes in underbrush.

"My Uncle Vicente, he had one boy, 'bout four years old," Dad said. "It wintertime and two feet snow on the ground. My uncle, he get on one horse to find de sheep. His boy, he chase after him. But daddy, he didn' know dat and momma, she thought de boy with daddy. So uncle, he come home, and momma, she ask, 'Where's de boy?' They look and look for him, but couldn' find him. Dey go here and dere, everywhere, no boy. Pretty soon, dey find him in one snowbank, froze to death. Poor boy."

"He was your cousin," I said.

"Dat's right. Yours too."

"What did Uncle Vicente do?"

"What can he do?" Dad said. "He sad and momma, she cry and cry. Dey bury de boy and den dey go back to work. Can't do noding else. If uncle stop workin' den whole ranch go down, down and he can't eat, or momma, she can't eat, and so no use cryin.' Can't change noding. God, He got one book, and if He look in de book and He fin' your name, den it don' matter. Nodin' you can do."

"You've told me about God's Book, Dad."

"Dat's right!"

Gazing out the window, he suddenly yelled, "Stop! Stop!"

"What?" I slid on the dirt road.

"You see dat building dere?"

I nodded and Jess pressed his face between our seats to see.

"I live dere for three months one winter. I think '51 or '52, don' 'member. Cold as a sonofabitch! Worst cold. Can't believe it. Never been so cold."

Record levels of snow had fallen in March 1952, leaving ranchers, herders, and livestock stranded and starving. Both federal and state authorities under

Operation Haylift dropped bales of hay to curtail livestock deaths. Thousands lived that might have died.

Built into a hillside, the house had a thatched and sagging roof with walls more than a foot thick made of adobe bricks.

"I build one fire inside to keep warm. Den in de morning, I come out and count de sheep to see how many alive. Some of dem, dey freeze. Sheep, dey get in a circle to keep warm, so some on de outside, dey don' make it. Maybe a coyote, he come and eat dem, and if he don,' den I butcher one and cook it and eat it."

An expansive field opened across the road from the house. At one end, two large hills faced each other with a shallow valley between. Nature had fashioned a wind tunnel that channeled cold air into a narrow passage and magnified the depth of temperature and the intensity of blizzards. What the earth had created here, the best scientists would have had difficulty reproducing in the laboratory. Nature had taken her time and made it perfect.

"I had to take the sheep out from dere. The snow, it over five feet. You only see de top of dem fence posts dere. But you got only couple hours. If you go before, it too cold and you lose fingers or toes. If you go after, same ding. But two hours not enough to get sheep through de snow and more die every day. So what you can do?"

"You lose your fingers and toes," said Jess from the back.

"Gotta save yourself," I said. "Better them than you."

"Oh come on! You no much a sheepherder."

"No, I'm not, Dad."

Jess laughed.

"What did you do?"

"I wait for one truck to plow de snow and den—slow, slow—I follow behind and de sheep, dey come behind me."

"Well, you didn't say a truck was coming."

"I didn' know."

"How was that an option then?"

"Dings, dey just work out. Little faith, dat's all. I need one truck and it come. When you out dere herdin' sheep, you need water and over dere, over de next hill you find it, or if rain comin' down hard, it stop."

"Oh, for heaven's sake. Hoping for a snowplow doesn't make it come."

"Why not?" He smiled.

"Things work out," Jess volunteered.

Their subtle mysticism derived from a pattern of adaptability, a way of accepting hardship and turning it instantly into solutions for immediate problems. Had the truck not arrived to plow the road, Dad would have told a different story of how he had saved the sheep by bringing them into the adobe house or finding a cave to shield them from the wind. Dad did not really hope for a snowplow. The truck simply arrived and he adapted to take advantage of it.

In a much larger sense, the Basques had confronted numerous obstacles on the road of history—linguistic, religious, cultural—and they had clung firmly to old ways, or absorbed the obstacle, turned it, made it their own, and adapted by it—a handy tool for survival.

Our Suburban bumped along the dirt road until we came to a gate. Its sign read NO TRESPASSERS. Jess got out, unhooked the barbed-wire loop from the fence post, and swung the gate open. I crossed the forbidden barrier.

"Dis was my uncle Vicente's ranch. Dis de first place I work when I come here. He got hard time, my uncle."

"How so?"

"Dey got de depression all over de world. My daddy, he come 1910 and again 1920 to help brother. Dey do pretty good. Den depression and good-bye, Charlie. All de cattle, all de sheep. Dey butcher dem or sell dem, and you can't get not one goddamn dime for one cow. Nobody got any money."

"That's a pretty tough lesson, Dad."

"You betcha, and den Uncle Vicente, he give up. He got one dream and den dat goddamn depression take it all away."

"Not all of it. He kept the house, didn't he?"

"Dat's all. Dey almos' starve to death. When I come here, he not got half de sheep he got before. Dat almos' twenty years later."

"What did you do when you got your first paycheck?"

"I go to Elko and put it in de bank. Got to save for one ranch my own, or one house. I keep a few dollars for drinks and food. I don' spend noding because I don' got noding."

A couple hundred feet inside the forbidden zone, we came to an abandoned house with three walls made of pine logs each a foot thick. The ends were cut and fit together like jigsaw puzzle pieces, which limited the need for nails and made the structure exceptionally strong and durable. A hillside served as a fourth wall, blending the house into the landscape next to a grove of trees.

"Dis, my room." Dad showed me inside. It resembled a walk-in closet. He had slept on the ground with a rollaway of blankets and a wad of clothes for a pillow.

"Pretty nice room," Jess said.

"Here, one wood-burnin' stove." He pointed to an outline on the floor where something heavy had once rested outside his room. Overhead a hole in the ceiling showed an outlet for a chimney.

"What happened to it?" I asked.

"It been sold or stolen. Noding else here worth anyding."

The house had been ransacked at some point since Dad left in 1957. Covering the wooden floor were three or four layers of paper—letters from a soldier to his mother, a few graded homework assignments, a box of eight-track tapes, and an IMPEACH NIXON sign. Other histories crossed in this place, and each one offered special meaning to those left behind.

I wondered if the mother who received the letters or her soldier son who sent them understood how valuable they might become four decades after they had been written and received. Those letters had the capacity to conjure stories—important stories—of a son's voice and a mother's tears. Did the son return from Vietnam? If not, I wondered if the mother could feel the ghostly embrace of her boy by the handwritten words scrawled down the page. The letters chronicled a past, an important history written from one generation to another, that deserved to be read and honored and protected and, most of all, remembered. But the letters remained strewn underfoot, muddy and torn. Nature would consign them eventually to mulch.

I thought of the Basques in that moment, of stories told by Dad and his generation that piled up in my head, stories that seemed to them like ordinary pieces of conversation and rarely found their way into print, but to me and others offered depth and richness to a people with an epic past that stretched back before Christ and spanned multiple continents. Would these stories suffer the same fate as the emotional letters from Vietnam? I worried that the answer would be yes. I thought then of the few old people of Gernika, reaching into their eighties or nineties, symbols of their generation, whom I had seen snoozing on park benches, and it occurred to me that as each of them died, now several per year, their stories too turned to nature's mulch, and a thread of history wound its way into oblivion.

Outside, Dad headed to a smaller building.

"Damn thing, it smell de same," he said. One whiff and the structure screamed chicken coop. After half a century, these ghostly chickens still left their stench in the world.

"May we all make such a lasting mark," I said.

"Over dere, dat's a blacksmith. My uncle, he shoe de horses, sharpen de knives and axes."

"Did you ever ride horseback to herd sheep?"

"No, no. Use one horse for cows. With sheep, you walk and walk. You gotta be alongside dem. One go here or dere, den you got to bring 'em back. If one go over a hill, dey all go over de hill. Don't know why. Around here, if one sheep go across one big creek, pretty soon all dem go over and den you got to get dem back. If it cold and dey get wet, den dey freeze at night, and den good-bye, Charlie."

"And if you get wet?"

"That's good-bye, Charlie too," Jess chimed in.

Dad paused, out of breath from age and excitement, and his hands went to his hips. A silence covered the world, a moment when we closed our eyes to listen and, hearing nothing, stretched our ears. We made out a creek in the distance gurgling through broken ice, the whisk of breeze enveloping tree and rock and brush, and the running of water somewhere nearby. A world within a world awaited a peeling away to find the simple and sweet and natural underneath. It was always there, covered by chaos, but at the core, serenity.

Dad followed the sound of running water. We came to an eight-foot steel trough, fully settled as though it had grown there like a metal weed. A pipe poured water into it and the overflow drained down to the bottom of the hill where a garden had once been cultivated by the residents of the house.

"You see dis pipe?"

I nodded.

"I help Uncle Vicente put dis pipe here fifty years ago." He pointed to a hill in the distance. "De water, it come from one spring way up dere and dis water never end. It keepa goin' and goin'."

I said nothing. Today such an act would not only require permits but might even be illegal if the spring originated on public land. Regardless, the freshness of the air and Dad's giddiness made me sentimental. I saw the water as the bedrock of life—the simplicity of its origins, the honesty of its flow, the goodness of its purpose.

Simplicity showed all around; it felt permanent, not fleeting. It defined us. How we worked, with joy or resentment, showed our heart; how we honored truth, with reluctance or reverence, showed our character; and how we served others, grudgingly or expectantly, showed our fate as a species. So many focused on complex things when simple things mattered more.

Staring at the gush from the pipe, Dad said, "Dhis been running for fifty years now and it run for five hundred if you don' touch it."

We came around the house and saw a camper trailer on the other side with a sawed-off flatbed painted camouflage brown and covered in a military tarp of dark green.

"What de hell dat camper dere?"

"I don't know. Maybe someone is living out here."

We looked in the camper, but no one was home. Outside the door, blue cardboard drawers stood in four columns with labels reading EXPLOSIVES, EXPLOSIVE CAPS, CABLE, ASSORTED PARTS, PUDDY.

I looked again at the camouflage wagon and thought that we had stumbled on a militia hideout or a weekend encampment, a place where gun-toting patriots came to hone their military skills between swigs of beer in case the United Nations or Al Qaeda tried to invade the mining and ranching communities of Nevada.

"We better be going," I told Dad and Jess, hoping not to meet whoever owned the trailer and wagon.

Dad looked one last time at his first home in America, admiring the house, trough, chicken coop, and collapsed barn. He turned to the field opposite that gradually sloped into a valley below.

"Look at dis fuckin' place. Dis green field once, far as you could see. Not anymore. Now just brush and dirty. No water. No nodin'."

Looking over the prairie valley, feeling Dad's nostalgia and the serenity all round, I realized clearly how far he had traveled, not merely from one continent to another, but from one station of life to another. He had no material wealth, but a wealth of dignity, a currency infinitely more valuable, longer-lasting, and honorable. It derived from having nothing—a man stripped bare of all in this world. But left only with strong hands and a big heart and a deep yearning to be more, to achieve more, to be better, he struggled and worked to look back in his final days to see a life well lived and a span of goodly labor from beginning to end. The journey mattered more than the destination.

Dad's story, I thought, was a very American story. Standing on that hill next to him and Jess, I thought of the simplicity of our Republic and how Dad had followed the blueprint as well as any man could, finding life and liberty, and pursuing happiness through toil and sweat. He worried about a next meal, exerted his back against unlimited work, and ached as he turned in at night to stare at black skies streaked with infinite stars. He fought to succeed and defied death on occasion. Yet somehow he seemed happy, quite happy, for a man who had endured a greater share of obstacles than most. He had no guarantees of happiness—only the opportunity to pursue it—but what I realized on that windswept mound was that the pursuit offered more pleasure in retrospect than the happiness itself, and any credit for his final station in life therefore accrued in equal parts to him and to his adopted American home.

From the perch overlooking the field, Dad climbed into the truck as Jess unhooked and rehooked the NO TRESPASSERS gate. Driving away, he glanced back.

"Jus' old now. Everyding jus' get old and dried up."

"Everything gets old, Dad. It changes all the time, but nothing dries up if we remember it."

"But I forget sometimes," he said.

"Well, I won't forget and I won't let you either."

The Suburban bumped down the dirt road, raising a plume of dust behind us.

# 20

Tía Pilar packed a sack with breakfast pastries and breads, meats, and cheeses for lunch. Our drive to Bilbao required three hours depending on traffic, but she stocked us with enough food and drink for a week.

I loved that woman, so warmhearted and full of light and goodwill. At seventy-four years old, she still saw life and the world through a child's eyes— simple and adventurous—never casting off the joy and innocence that so many shed early in life in exchange for cynicism and doubt. With her, all was possible; her dreams did not shrink.

"I'll miss you," I told her.

She kissed my cheeks and hugged me, and told Tío Pedro to kiss and hug me too, which he dutifully did like an automaton. Then she kissed and hugged me a second time. I rolled around in the joy and warmth.

Dad hugged her with big arms. Pulling apart and holding his cheeks in her hands, she kissed him as tears welled up but did not fall. She gave way to a third round of kisses and hugs for me, and a second for Dad before scooting us out the door with our sack of food.

In the Subaru, Dad sat quiet for miles. Like Tía Pilar, his tears did not fall, but they seeped out from the corners of his eyes, awaiting a subtle push from a strong emotion or a replay of events in the foyer of her home.

"What are you thinking about?" I asked after some time had passed.

"You 'member when Amy born?"

"Of course I do."

"What you 'member?"

"I was twelve. We sat in the hospital waiting for the doctor or nurse. The nurse came out with Amy just out of Mom and she handed her to you. You said, 'She cry a lot,' and then you said, 'She purple,' and she most certainly was. They let you carry her to the nursery before seeing Mom. That was the first time I ever saw you cry."

Dad said nothing.

"What makes you think of that?"

"Oh, I don' know. It come to me, some reason," he said. "Where we go now?"

"We're going to Lekeitio to see Tía Anita and Tía Juanita, and then tonight we drive to Bilbao and fly home tomorrow."

In Lekeitio, we bumped the Subaru along cobblestone to pass the church formidably ensconced behind bronze doors and towering above everything else. Next to it a market by the harbor buzzed with life. Fishermen had begun arranging tables with cod and squid and clams and other catches from the day. Such simplicity between them: the market fed their bellies, the church their souls, and the two offered a liturgy of life that had carried Lekeitio, and the Basques, from one generation to the next.

"We can go see your mom and dad's graves," I reminded him as we passed the stone stairs leading up to the dark briar of tree limbs and thorny bushes.

"No, no," he whispered, and I didn't press him.

"We need one store," he said suddenly.

"For what?"

"We buy someding for Anita and Juanita before we go dere."

"What do you want to buy?"

"I show you. You go down here," and I turned as he told me.

He looked searchingly but didn't seem to find what he wanted.

"It no here, or someplace else. I don' 'member." His hands shook and I grabbed them and held them.

"Dad, what do you need? Let me help you. What do you want?"

"One chocolate."

"I see. We'll find some chocolate. Don't worry. We'll find it. Calm down."

In a few blocks, I parked and went inside a small bakery, but didn't find chocolate.

"You got it?" Dad's tone was panicked.

"No," I said reluctantly.

"We need to find," and his tone grew to physical agitation.

"She gave me directions. I know where to go."

Inside another bakery, an assortment of chocolates lined up next to baked bread, croissants, and pastries, all made that morning, fresh and warm, a tease for the nose. I bought two bags of chocolate and two bouquets of daisies and tulips.

"Dis good!" Dad said excitedly, and a smile of relief as much as joy came to his face. His eyes lit up and his hands stopped shaking.

When we arrived at the nursing home, his hands shook again and I had to hold the chocolate and the flowers as we buzzed in.

"Calm down. It'll be okay."

"I nervous."

"About what?"

"I don' know."

The residents hadn't congregated for lunch, so we walked down the hall to find Tía Juanita's room. She sat in a chair, her arm limp, half her face melting off the bone. Her hair glistened a deep black though the center part showed white roots.

Dad gave her a bouquet and chocolates and she studied him as she had before. Recollection came sooner this time, and she grabbed his hand with her good arm. He hugged and kissed her. Setting the chocolates aside, she inhaled the daisies and tulips deeply, as if neither she nor her room had seen a sign of the world in a long time.

"Back to America?" she gurgled.

"Yes, tomorrow," he said.

Tía Juanita nodded and then looked ahead, admiring nothing, like the old people of Gernika who sat on benches in the city center.

I filled a glass with water and set the flowers in it.

Her drooping eyes stared through me and then, reaching again with her good arm, she tried to pucker and kiss my cheeks, but lacked the control or strength for either.

We sat in silence, allowing her to feel our presence and showing our love and respect in the only way left to express it.

Dad touched her arms and face and kissed her a last time—a last time.

"She not be 'round long," he told me in the hallway.

"Probably true, Dad." I put my arm around him. "But you've seen her off, and that's a nice thing."

"No Bascos 'round long too."

I pulled my arm harder around his shoulders and didn't say anything.

We went up a floor to Tía Anita and poked our head around the door-frame. She sat on the bed, white kerchief in hand, brushing her dark brown hair, which showed no sign of original roots. A white clip held the hair behind her ear like a schoolgirl's hairdo. She sensed in her brushing a familiarity but seemed unaware of the motion, and had we not come along, she would have stroked the brush a thousand times more until the strands pulled out.

"Kaixo!" He startled her in Euskara from a distant dream.

"Dad, wait a second. Let her adjust," I told him.

She turned to me, back to Dad, and then smiling wide, she came off the bed to embrace him as strongly and boldly as she had on the first day. She remembered him, and I saw again in her face a soliloquy of *never letting go, never again, never again,* and I became sentimental. Her tears came and she blew her nose and it sounded like Dad all over again.

"Who this?" she asked of me.

"Dis my son. You know him."

"What his name?"

"Vicente."

"What?"

"Vicente. You know dat name."

"I do?" she asked, puzzled.

"You do," Dad assured her. But she didn't and Dad knew that.

Appearing disappointed, he took her to the bed and sat next to her. He handed the daisies and tulips over and like Tía Juanita, she shut her eyes and inhaled the perfume to deepen the sensation. Then opening the bag, she pulled out a chocolate and bit into it.

She stared ahead and a glaze came to her eyes as she chewed, the same glaze that trapped her in the hairbrush dream, one that couldn't be shaken unless interrupted or the chocolate disappeared.

She reached in the bag for a second piece, and when it was nearly to her mouth, she stopped short and gave it to Dad instead, and together they ate chocolates side by side, and I saw them as scruffy children sharing contraband under the nose of Franco's soldiers.

———

I wondered why Dad had thought of Amy's birth after leaving Tía Pilar, and why he had panicked while in search of chocolate, and why his hands had shaken at the nursing home. At the time, he didn't know why he had behaved as he did, and honestly, neither did I, nor can I be certain now.

But if I had guessed, I would have said that each of us holds only a handful of dear, precious memories, the kind that define us, shape us, the ones that we carry for a lifetime from place to place and cling to when all else falls apart—a broken arm, a tricycle, cut-bite-pull, a dance, a donkey, a crucifix, a piece of chocolate. These few precious moments—for there are only a few—get stored up in a special part of the mind, where we can get at them and protect them, like a mother peeking into a room to make sure her babies are safe.

If ever a moment gains passage, it triggers recollection of the few others that reside there, how a song reminds us of a wedding day, or a scent of tobacco takes us to a barbershop, or the sight of blood transports us to a meat counter or a butcher block in a backyard.

The experiences of leaving Tía Pilar and seeing his twin had inched their way into Dad's special place, where they now sit along with Amy's birth, an event late in Dad's life when he had nervously taken on the challenges of a newborn, a task infinitely more demanding than birthing a lamb. The memories seemed to be of beginnings and endings, bookends of life, a special birth and the last embrace of a twin before God runs a finger down a gold leaf page to find her name in His book.

In our same hotel, the Palacio Urgoiti in Mungia outside Bilbao, Dad settled in with his remote, took his pills, and fell asleep. I watched him snore quietly, peacefully in the night, and knew that he dreamt old dreams, but I hoped he dreamt new ones too.

From nowhere, our old barn popped into my head. I recalled hammering nails on a hot tin roof and hearing him tell me at the end, "It good idea you go to college," and feeling afterward as though nothing in the world lay beyond my reach.

After high school, I had returned home to deliver a letter to my parents, one that admitted me to Harvard at the Kennedy School of Government.

"What de name of dat school?" Dad had asked as Mom danced around the house and began calling friends and relatives to announce the news.

"Harvard."

"No, no, de oder one."

"You mean, Kennedy School?"

"Dat's de one—Kennedy." He had exaggerated the pronunciation.

He then put on his glasses and took the envelope into the sun. Touching the thick paper, the words, the insignia, he had little idea what it said. From across the room, I watched him move his fingers over the raised lettering, as he had done as a boy in a Lekeitio schoolhouse, tilting the paper into the shining light, and then when finished, pulling the glasses from his face and wiping his eyes with the back of his hand.

Watching him sleep now, as he had watched me in the small apartment of the Blue Jay Bar, I thought of the duty that a son owes his mother and father, knowing there are differences between them. To a mother, a son owes kindness to the world, helpful hands, shoulders of comfort and warmth, and compassion manifest each day through common acts and a way of life. Then a mother can say of her son that she taught him well, showed him to love and to be good to others, and by his small deeds, to let others rely on him and he on them, making the world better for it. This duty flows naturally from a mother's earnest heart, her maternal bosom, and a son pulls it in and absorbs it and makes it part of himself and passes it on and keeps faith with the warm knowledge and holds no malice or contempt for having it. Beauty and simplicity billow forth in the transference.

But a son's duty to a father is far more complicated. It travels through many boundaries, a need to obey and gain acceptance, a yearning as a child to make a father proud, and falling short again and again, finally acquiescing to the fact that he cannot sate a father's pride. Such realization turns to shame and then anger, and soon rebellion fills the void. Here a danger lurks if revolt turns a son to destruction and then any joy once shared between father and son evaporates and hollows out the heart of both.

The better path brings the son out from under his father and lets him chart a parallel course, one imprinted by the father's voice and seared by the father's shadow, but wholly the property of the son. On this new trajectory, the son carves his way, believing that all actions and deeds are his own, that he moves one way or another without influence from anyone, and he needs no affirmation, certainly not his father's. He goes boldly forth until a day comes when he finds in himself the voice and shadow of his father and he does not want to believe it. But there it is and there it stays and he cannot shake it anymore than he can hack off an arm or a leg, and so he accepts it and he smiles for the clarity of duty that finally descends upon him—to honor thy father and to respect his origin and the hard fragments of his past, and in so doing, to embrace the voice and shadow in himself. And when the father turns to ash and dust, the son knows the transfer to be complete and feels the older living on inside the younger.

——✺——

In the early morning, darkness still enveloped Mungia, but I woke to Dad's rumbling nose, as I had so often in life, and I laughed again, knowing that his snotty sound was stored impenetrably somewhere in the recesses of my brain, like my very own chocolate, probably satisfying and sweet only to me.

On the plane, I said, "Are you glad you came back home?"

"I not come home. I goin' home now," he replied, pointing westward across the ocean en route to America.

"You think you'll ever come back?"

"No more. Good visit. Dis last time, dough. You know—" He paused. "You momma and sisters, dey goin' to be mad at you."

"I know, Dad. I knew that before we came."

"Maybe you stay in Spain. Dat safer." And then he laughed.

"Don't worry. That'll be my cross to bear."

Any nagging conscience over deceiving Mom, Jonna, and Amy had melted away after seeing Dad and Tía Anita together, if not the first time, then certainly the second.

Sister Mary Kathleen's gruff spiritual voice had lost its hold, and Sister Dennis's cherubic apparition now hugged me without malice.

Come what may in life or the hereafter, my sin, motivated by love and guided by goodness, received a full pardon.

Rejoining two hearts, igniting bliss, making dreams manifest—to do less would have been unforgivable.

# Afterwards

"She so good," Dad said of Tía Juanita.

Nearly a year to the day after our surprise visit to Spain, Dad's sister died of heart complications in the Lekeitio nursing home.

"How do you feel?" I asked him.

"I okay. Little sad, but I say good-bye last year."

I didn't say anything.

"Thank you," he then said to me, a rare moment.

"You're very welcome, Dad."

I thought of Sister Mary Kathleen and Sister Dennis and wondered now what they might have thought about my original deception. But it no longer mattered to me. I had made peace with it.

Three months after Tía Juanita, Chapo died at age eighty of a heart attack. His son found him lying on the couch, fast asleep. The family asked me to write the obituary for the local paper, which I sadly did, penning each heavy word and thinking of a hundred others to describe this small man who had been such an integral part of my childhood and memory.

Chapo came from Gizaburuaga, his birthplace, in 1954 and herded sheep for several ranching outfits in the valleys and foothills of Elko County. He ate from cans or fished in streams, and he slept by campfires, enduring scorching summers and the coldest of winters, but he prided himself on not losing a herd and working from sunup to sundown without complaint or regret about leaving Spain and coming to America.

A few days before he died, he had served as head chef at the Elko Basque Festival, his round belly wrapped in a white apron emblazoned with the very important title "Chef Chapo." Friends saw him wearing a straw hat and barking orders to turn the steaks, toss the salad, stir the beans, and find the plates for over a thousand people in attendance. All were served—orderly, efficiently.

Chapo played *mus* up to the last week of his life. No one ever imagined that a card game could produce an aerobic workout, but Chapo took his *mus* playing seriously and managed to raise his blood pressure during each match.

Neither cooking nor playing *mus* offered him the immense joys of fishing. He spent as much time casting a line at South Fork or Dorsey Reservoir in Elko County, or huddling near a beaver dam in Lamoille Canyon, as he did behind a grill or seated at a card table. "His favorite fishing spot," said Dad, "was the one with the most fish." Naturally, he cooked and ate everything he caught, or wrapped the fish and gave them to friends for a healthy lunch. Sometimes he even went over and cooked the fish for them.

"Do you miss Chapo?" I asked Dad.

"No, I don't—yes, I do," he said.

"Make up your mind. Which is it?"

"Dey all dying, dat's all. Every last one of dem."

"It'll be okay, Dad."

"You sure?" he asked.

"I'm sure, Dad," and I knew the Basques as a people would carry on.

# Acknowledgments

When undertaking a first book, the greatest hurdle is self-confidence. Can I write a book? If I do, will the writing be good enough? Do I risk personal embarrassment from lack of skill? I don't avoid challenge merely to avoid failure, not at all. On the contrary, I learn a great deal from my failures, but I also don't shine bright lights on them. In the end, these concerns compelled me to keep this book a secret, even from most family and friends, until it neared actual publication.

I finished the manuscript in about six weeks. Only then did I share it with a circle of friends—two brutal friends, in fact—the kind who know writing, both the good and the bad, and would gladly tell me how horribly I had misjudged my own writing prowess. To Bob Muldoon and Cris Watkins, I offer my thanks for not sparing my feelings, for offering truth, and for knowing that our friendship remains strong enough to withstand any constructive criticism. I look forward to reviewing their first books and returning the favor with equal care and brutality.

As I put the final touches on the manuscript, I enlarged my circle by three, people close to me, who offered encouragement and love, cheered my progress, and pressed me to finish the book even when my attention or energy waned. A best friend of mine, Mikel Lopategui, who found his way into these pages, remained as reliable and trusting as in our first days building tree houses in childhood. My English teacher from high school, Cathy Smales, gave warmth and enthusiasm, a potent combination that she sprinkles over all of her students, both present and past. Anita Williams, my mom's sister, my aunt and surrogate grandmother, became a quiet confidante, allowing me to share frustration and vent anxiety.

In August 2010, I had finished my first round of revisions for the University of Nevada Press. At the same time, the U.S. State Department asked me to undertake a mission in Afghanistan to help America's war effort. Initially, I was apprehensive, believing myself ill-suited for the top secret task. But told that "your country is asking you to do this," I could not refuse.

With my departure imminent, I faced the possibility that I might not return from Afghanistan. Still, for Dad's sake, I had to make sure the work made it through publication, even if I wasn't around, so I again expanded my circle by two—Richard Urey and Loni Nannini. Both of them agreed to shepherd the manuscript over the finish line if I couldn't do so myself. My instruction to them was simple: make sure that Dad sees the book and that Mom reads the book. I thank them immeasurably for their generosity.

Finally, I extend great thanks to the University of Nevada Press, especially Margaret Fisher Dalrymple, who thoughtfully reviewed the manuscript, suggested improvements, and brought it to fruition. Margaret is an exceptionally warm and kind person and a credit to the university system and to the whole State of Nevada. She shared the manuscript with a couple of anonymous reviewers, who kindly helped with Basque spellings and offered wonderful advice to navigate between subtle controversies in Basque academia and culture that might have unnecessarily detracted from the main narratives of the book. My final appreciation goes to Jan McInroy, who patiently copyedited the book, drawing her sharp sword to cut down dangling modifiers, subtle or blatant inconsistencies, and the occasional lapse in grammar.

Overall, I could not have asked for a warmer, more thoughtful group of people to help guide this first book to final print and into publication. I am eternally grateful to all of them.